A Collection distributed by Heron Books

WOMEN
WHO
MADE
HISTORY

Boadicea contemplating suicide
after defeat by the Romans

BOADICEA

BY
J. M. SCOTT

Distributed by
HERON BOOKS

CONTENTS

LIST OF ILLUSTRATIONS

EDITOR'S FOREWORD

In 55 B.C. Julius Caesar, bold general that he was, made an incursion into England, then a little-known island on the edge of the Roman world. He tried again the next year, employing a fleet of over 800 ships, but when he left to return to his fate in Rome, the British tribes, a relatively civilized people, went thankfully back to their old barbarian ways. But their freedom was not to last. In 43 A.D. the Romans finally swarmed onto the island in force and gradually conquered it. After the legions came the speculators, and as was usual with the Romans in a newly-conquered province, they squeezed the natives for all they could get.

In 60 A.D. the proud British tribes, still only half subjugated, reacted convulsively. There was a brief and terrible rebellion, led by an obscure native queen: Boadicea—but even her desperate efforts were no match for the stubborn and methodical Romans. In a final battle, in which it is said some 80,000

Britons perished, the revolt was crushed. The Romans were to stay on in Britain for another 350 years.

Thus Boadicea appeared and disappeared from history—all in one short year. She left little concrete evidence of her struggle behind her, silent witnesses to war, invasion and agony. In the Roman towns of Colchester and St. Albans, which she sacked, excavations have revealed deep layers of ash and burnt clay. In Colchester the remains of a gutted pottery shop have been found beneath a café on the High Street with fragments of hundreds of smashed Samian bowls, burnt black, and great lumps of fused glass fragments. Another site has revealed piles of scrap metal where the terrified inhabitants of the doomed town had been desperately making weapons and armour just before the final, ferocious assault of Boadicea's hordes. The enraged tribesmen had hacked away the face of a Roman soldier on a tombstone, and had torn off the head of an equestrian statue of Claudius in the great temple of the city, had carried it off more than forty miles and had dumped it in the river Alde, where it was found many centuries later.

Yet the legend of Boadicea, as J.M. Scott

shows in this perceptive study, has lived on lustily for many centuries right up to our own. Perhaps it was because she was a woman, and a queen at that. There may be a parallel in Zenobia, Queen of Palmyra, a caravan state in the Syrian desert, who was also a widow and revolted unsuccessfully against Rome in 270 A.D. But it is doubtful if even even Zenobia—though far richer and more civilized than Boadicea—is as well remembered as our queen, at least among the British.

Even today the name of this queen about whom so little is known is recognized in all the lands where English is spoken. Ever since the British could call themselves a separate people Boadicea has been lovingly remembered and cherished as the first and most romantic of British heroines. She appeals to British nationalism. Historically, her career may have lasted for hardly twelve months, yet she has lived in history for close on two thousand years.

Courtlandt Canby
Editor of the Series

PREFACE

Boadicea is remembered, more than nineteen centuries after her death, as one of the most romantic figures in our island story. This is remarkable for several reasons, apart from the great span of time.

The only historians who can have any claim to contemporary knowledge of the events concerned are Roman writers—who must be considered as the enemy. However objective they tried to be one cannot expect them to describe her and her actions sympathetically; and they do not. Many hundreds of years were to pass before a British account appeared, and by that time this island must have been thoroughly indoctrinated with the Roman point of view.

Then, we know so little about her personally. There is only one quite short description of her appearance. That is certainly impressive. But we know almost nothing about her early life. At the time of her rebellion, when there is first mention of her, she was a widow with two young daughters. She was beaten by the Romans, her daughters were raped and her people dispossessed. She rose against the oppressors, gathering other tribes to her standard. Thereafter, for a few months at most, her followers behaved with a savagery which is shocking even by the standards of the time. Her followers sacked three Roman-dominated towns and Boadicea came near to driving across the sea the army of the greatest empire in the world. Then, when the odds were numerically very much in her favour, she was routed—and disappears from history by an unknown end, while what remained of her people suffered the consequences.

There are points both good and bad in this, to attract and to repel. But is there enough of the former to create a national heroine? The fact remains that Boadicea is in that category. And the sceptic is entitled to wonder whether she had been "built up" by fact or fiction, history or legend.

Let us enumerate the points which have made her name remembered, without at this stage separating the legendary from the authenticated. The first is childish, literally so. It is in our schooldays that almost all of us learn our ancient history. This is uninspiring to the schoolboy. Then he comes upon a person—a woman!—who rose against the Romans and dashed about in a chariot with scythes on the axles cutting off the legs of the people whose dead language he has to endure in other uninspiring lessons. That is something he remembers for the rest of his life! He may have acquired no more information about the lady, but that is enough.

The writer cannot speak with the same authority about schoolgirls. It is possible that Boadicea has for them a less bloodthirsty and more feminist appeal. And certainly a woman warrior can be a romantic image for any adult—unless he happens actually to have met a female revolutionary. In the more exalted plane, Joan of Arc was our enemy, but she is admired in this country scarcely less than in France.

Then, Boadicea rose against oppression, against an omnipotent conqueror. That has a very strong appeal, bolstering national pride. Such defiance has inspired our finest emotions, our best prose. As Lewis Spence wrote in 1937: "If the fire of her rebellion glows like a torch at the gateway of our history, it continues to burn because of the deathless and intrepid patriotism which lit and inspired it."

3

Winston Churchill in his *History of the English-Speaking Peoples* described the burdens and abuses which led up to the revolt, and wrote: "There followed an uprush of hatred from the abyss, which is a measure of the cruelty of the conquest. It was a scream of rage against invincible oppression and the superior culture which seemed to lend it power.... Her monument on the Embankment opposite Big Ben reminds us of the harsh cry 'Liberty or Death' which has echoed down the ages."

As for the horrors, they happened long enough ago for us to accept them with far less revulsion than we would feel at some minor cruelty read of in today's newspaper. But, paradoxically, a heroic or dramatic act keeps its value irrespective of time and distance—and *almost* irrespective of accuracy. If a story has sufficient heroism and drama it will go on moving people from generation to generation, whether it be true, not quite true, or downright fiction.

The story of Boadicea's rebellion has dramatic quality. No doubt about that. But is this sufficient in itself to explain its survival? And in what proportions does it depend on facts and on legend? The historical sources are limited. The most trustworthy and illuminating

4

is Tacitus. His father-in-law, Agricola, was in Britain at the time of the rebellion, and Tacitus heard the story from his lips. Tacitus is a careful historian, unconvicted by scholars of any deliberate false statement in his records. He gives a short account in his *Agricola* and a longer one in his *Annals*. The other main classical source is Cassius Dio, or Dion, who was born in about 155 A.D.—some ninety-five years after the rebellion. For his account, which is at greater length, he evidently drew on Tacitus, but he may have had other contemporary sources which have been lost. If there is no corroboration for much that he says, in addition to what Tacitus has told us, at least it all fits in with our background knowledge. This background knowledge is uneven but in some fields adequate. We have from Roman sources plenty of information about the Roman civil and military organization, and a certain amount about the British tribes. Added to this are very considerable archaeological discoveries, many directly concerned with the Iceni, Boadicea's tribe. Thus it is possible to sift out a fairly detailed story which may be taken as historically true.

The plan of this book is to start with a chapter on the legend, giving the unauthenticated and frankly fictional versions. The remaining chapters tell the actual story— history borne out and expanded by archaeology. We begin with the scene in Britain at the beginning of the first century. In this we are to a certain extent helped by Julius Caesar's account of his two deep raids of 55 and 54 B.C. Then comes the invasion by Claudius of 43 A.D., the partial conquest, the beginnings of colonisation. Then the build-up and out-burst of rebellion; and finally its course and aftermath. The object is to give Boadicea's story a proper setting in history—a beginning, a middle and an end. Whether this contains the necessary dramatic ingredients, the reader must decide for himself.

One final point. Recorded history has given us facts to go on. Archaeology in the widest sense—digging up the past—has provided a wealth of data. But these facts and data are of comparatively little help in *seeing* a story without imagination—or deduction, which is imagination disciplined by facts. For instance, we know that a historical character did a certain thing. But to discover his or her motive, imagination must be used. The same is true for the interpretation of a find which science tells us is of appropriate date. So

imagination has been used here and there—
frankly and admitted as such—by the writer.
And it is still more necessary in the reader.

Scholars are now agreed that the person
with whom this book is concerned should be
named Boudicca, or perhaps Boudica, the
derivation being from the Welsh *buddug,* or
more ancient word *buddig*—both meaning
"victory."

Surely the main purpose in using a name is
to let people know to whom you are referring.
If our title were *Boudicca* some people would
recognize the subject and be satisfied that the
right word had been used. With *Boadicea* as
the title some may be critical. But at least
everyone will know whom the book is about.

For a similar reason I have generally referred
to Colchester, St. Albans, London, etc. instead
of Camulodunum, Verulamium, Londinium.
(For list see below.) But since the narrative is
inevitably peppered with the names of people
and tribes which have no modern equivalents
it has seemed best to simplify wherever possible.

For his background reading the writer is
chiefly indebted to the following books:
Boadicea, by Lewis Spence; *Roman Britain,* by

I. A. Richmond; *Roman Britain and the English Settlement*, by R. G. Collingwood and J. H. L. Myers; *The Rebellion of Boadicea*, by Donald R. Dudley and Graham Webster; and *The Roman Conquest of Britain*, by Donald R. Dudley and Graham Webster.

J. M. Scott

ROMAN NAMES OF PLACES
MENTIONED

Anglesey—Mona
Caernarvon—Sagontium
Canterbury—Durovernum
Chester—Deva
Colchester—Camulodunum
Exeter—Isca
Gloucester—Glevum
Isle of Man—Monavia
Lincoln—Lindum
London—Londinium
Richborough—Rutupiai
St. Albans—Verulamium
Silchester—Calleva
Staines—Pontes
Towcester—Lactodorum
Wall—Letocetum
Wroxeter—Viroconium

I

THE BUILDING
OF THE LEGEND

In the days when families played round games there was one which consisted of the telling of a story by the first player to the second, who repeated it to a third, who repeated it to a fourth—and so on until perhaps a dozen people had heard a version and then told their own. At the end the final result was compared with the original.

The story of Boadicea has been treated somewhat like that during the last nineteen hundred years.

Tacitus told it first, briefly as follows. Sixteen or seventeen years after the conquest of southern Britain in 43 A.D., Prasutagus, king of the Iceni, died. He left half of his considerable riches to his two daughters and the other half to the Emperor Nero, hoping thereby to win continued freedom for his kingdom. But the Roman chief Treasury official confiscated everything in the name of the Emperor, dispossessed the Icenian nobles and took many as slaves. His followers flogged the widow of Prasutagus, Boadicea, and raped her two daughters. This was the culmination of a long series of oppressions. The whole of south-east Britain rose in revolt under the leadership of Boadicea.

The Roman Governor, Suetonius Paulinus, was at that time engaged in the conquest of Anglesey and the north-western mainland of Wales. He at once rode to London with his cavalry, but before he felt strong enough to engage the British host, Boadicea had destroyed Colchester, London and St. Albans, and cut to pieces a strong legionary rescue force from Lincoln. In the final battle, however, the British were routed and Boadicea killed herself.

Dio Cassius repeated this story, adding further details. The only other classical historian concerned is Suetonius—the second century writer, not the Governor of Britain mentioned above. In the Dark Ages the voices of those writers were lost, not to be heard again until the Renaissance. During that period some strange tales passed as history. Even when the original sources could once more be consulted, a story which engaged the emotions as much as did that of Boadicea was handled in different ways, with variations of fact or emphasis. The Queen of the Iceni has by no

means always been treated as a heroine. It
may be useful, and it is certainly diverting, to
trace her ups and downs in popularity and the
various versions of her story. The final result
is in this case the original, borne out and
amplified—considerably amplified—by the
detective science of archaeology.

Gildas the Wise, born about 516, is our first
British historian. A monk and a saint, he was
chiefly concerned in pointing out the wickedness
of mankind in general and his own countrymen
in particular. For him the Romans, who had
been gone from this island for rather more
than a century, were the best of a bad lot. As
for his sources, he refers without naming
them to "foreign writers," but the chief value
of his *Liber querulus de excidio Britanniae* is as
a record of contemporary legend. From such
a writer we could hardly expect a complimentary
reference to Boadicea, and we do not get it.
But at least she is no worse castigated than
many other leaders:

"This island, stiff-necked and stubborn-
minded, from the time of its being first
inhabited, ungratefully rebels, sometimes
against God, sometimes against her own
citizens, and frequently, also, against foreign
kings and their subjects...

13

"For when the rulers of Rome had obtained the empire of the world, subdued all the neighbouring nations and islands towards the east, and strengthened their renown by the first peace which they made with the Parthians, who border on India, there was a general cessation from war throughout the whole world; the fierce flame which they kindled could not be extinguished or checked by the Western Ocean, but passing beyond the sea, imposed submission upon our island without resistance, and entirely reduced to obedience its unwarlike but faithless people, not so much by fire and sword and warlike engines, like other nations, but threats alone, and menaces of judgement frowning on their countenance, whilst terror penetrated to their hearts.

"When afterwards they returned to Rome, for want of pay, as is said, and had no suspicion of an approaching rebellion, that deceitful lioness [Boadicea], put to death the rulers who had been left among them, to unfold more fully, and to confirm the enterprises of the Romans. When the report of these things reached the Senate, and they with a speedy army made haste to take vengeance on the crafty foxes, as they called them, there was no

1. Boadicea, as seen through seventeenth century eyes, was a formidable matron. The story of her brave revolt has stirred British pride through many centuries.

2. Boadicea and her daughters, the famous statue group in London which has done much to perpetuate the legend of the British Queen.

3. Title-page of an eighteenth century tragedy based upon the ever-alluring legend of Boadicea. Many have bewailed the fact that Shakespeare never got around to writing a play on Boadicea.

BOADICIA.

A

TRAGEDY.

As it is acted at the

THEATRE-ROYAL

IN

DRURY-LANE.

By Mr. GLOVER.

LONDON:

Printed for R. and J. Dodsley in Pall-mall; and M. Cooper in Pater-noster-row. 1753.

(Price One Shilling and Six-pence.)

bold navy on the sea to fight bravely for the country; by land there was no marshalled army, no right wing of battle, nor other preparation for resistance; but their backs were their shields against their vanquishers, and they presented their necks to their swords, whilst chill terror ran through every limb, and they stretched out their hands to be bound, like women: so that it has become a proverb far and wide, that the Britons are neither brave in war, nor faithful in time of peace.

"The Romans, therefore, having slain many of the rebels, and reserved others for slaves, that the land might not be entirely reduced to desolation, left the island, destitute as it was of wine and oil, and returned to Italy, leaving behind them taskmasters, to scourge the shoulders of the natives, to reduce their necks to the yoke, and their soil to the vassalage of a Roman province."

A thousand years went by before Boadicea was again mentioned, for although Bede referred briefly to the rebellion in his *Ecclesiastical History* he did not name its leader. It remained for an Italian, Polydore Vergil, to write of "Voadicia" in his History of England. Apart from a few geographical errors (he confused the Isle of Anglesey, Mona, with the

Isle of Man) his account is reasonably accurate from the moment when the rebels "didde sodaynelie slide from the Romaines, in headlong rage with weapon rising against them," until their final defeat by Suetonius. Then, "Voadicia, cheefe governess of the battale, lest shee shoulde fall into the hands of her enimies, ended her life bie empoysoninge her selfe. The estate of the Ile from that time forth was more quiet."

Polydore Vergil spent most of his life in England, and it was at the wish of Henry VII that he undertook his history of Britain. He is adjudged by far the most scholarly and painstaking historian who wrote of England at that date. An interesting incident is that he asked James IV of Scotland for information on the Scottish kings. This request was refused on the grounds that only a Scotsman was suitable to write Scottish history. So this task was given to Hector Böece.

Böece (1465-1536) called Boadicea "Voada" and moved the scene of her rebellion a few hundred miles to the north. As with Polydore Vergil, the Isle of Anglesey is the Isle of Man. But most of the action is in Scotland. Berwick and Carlisle are destroyed by the rebels, and almost all the characters are Scottish.

"Voada send ane secrete servand to hir bruther Corbrede, king of Scottis, schawing the incredibill iniuries done to hir bi Romanis, hir dochteris brocht to sik calamite that pacience is bot place to mair displesour."

King Corbrede plays an important part. This is not the only occasion in the development of the legend when a man helps Boadicea. It is as if it could not be accepted that a woman had done so much on her own! But the ladies as a whole are often to the fore, for good and ill. When the Roman fortress of Carlisle was taken, "the Scottis were so kendillit in hatrent to revenge the iniuries done bi Romanis, that the wemen cessit fra na maner of cruelty that mycht be devisit aganis thame." And for the final battle, "Voada gadderit ane huge noumer of Britonis, with mony ladyis with manis corage in bricht harnes."

Böece describes the battle with fair accuracy. In fact there is a salting of truth throughout the whole account, enough to show that he had read Tacitus. But the magnet of nationalism pulled it all to the north.

Böece does, however, add a pleasant final touch. Though Voada kills herself, her two daughters are captured with weapons in their hands. And one of them marries a valiant Roman named Marius, "quhilk bereft hir virginite afoir." They became king and queen of Britain. One hopes that they lived happily ever after.

A few years after the death of Böece, Pietro Ubaldini came from his native Italy to England. He illustrated manuscripts, taught Italian, and fought in Scotland under Sir James Crofts in 1549. He was the author of *Vite delle Donne Illustre di Regno dell' Inghilterre e della Scotia*. A *Life* of one illustrious lady of the kingdom of England is that of Voadicia, and there is another of Bonduica—for Ubaldini has been confused by the various forms of Boadicea's name and the different versions of her story. He seems to have been listening to Tacitus, Dio and Böece talking all together. But this matters little, for he is less concerned with the details of a life story than with the moral that can be drawn from it. This, in translation, is what a critical Italian commented—of Voadicia: "...and thirty thousand men were cut to pieces, and thus was she constrained to yield up the country to her conquerors, and though adverse fortune had so cruelly reduced her from her former greatness to a state of extreme wretchedness, she nonetheless recalled her former nobility, and, in order that she might die free, not wishing to be paraded in triumph before her proud captors, she killed herself with poison, leaving for posterity the memory of a rare strength of character and a respected and generous wisdom."

And of Bonduica: "She was indeed worthy to be numbered among the great women of this kingdom because of her wondrous nobility, nor should the cruelty used by her towards her enemies be allowed to exclude her from that band of praiseworthy women when it was done on impulse and in the heat of revenge rather than as a manifestation of her natural inclination—either that or that the vices of the Roman soldiers, learnt from the wicked Nero, their Emperor, were such that they called for a punishment in keeping with their gravity."

Ubaldini was writing for Italians, who no doubt were as interested then as they are now in the eccentricities of British ladies. But he is of importance to the theme of this chapter because, like Böece with his happy ending, he provides something for the imagination to catch hold of. He widened the audience.

Edmund Spenser widened it still more in England. In *The Ruines of Time* Boadicea is:

Bunduca, that victorious Conqueresse
That lifting up her brave heroick thought
'Bove womens weakness, with the Romans fought:
Fought, and in field against them thrice prevailed.

In *The Faerie Queene* she fights the Romans on the Severn:

But being all defeated, save a few,
Rather than fly, or be captiv'd, her-selfe she slew.

Thus, during the reign of Queen Elizabeth, the queen of the Iceni is for the first time given the status of a heroine. But the audience was still small and comparatively sophisticated, limited to those who could read.

The next phase was the telling of the story visually and vocally. This brought it within the range of everyone—but at the price of drifting even further from the original, for historical drama is history as it *ought* to have been.

Ben Jonson included Boadicea in his *Masque of Queenes*. She appears eighth in an illustrious company of female rulers who range back into antiquity and legend. She is thus presented:

"'The eygt, our owne honor, Voadicea, by some Boadicia, by some Bunduica, and Bunduca: Queene of the Iceni, a people that inhabited that part of the Iland which was call'd East-Anglia... since she was borne here at home, we will first honor her with a home-borne testimony from the grave and diligent Spenser."

He quotes the verse given above, then gives specimens of what Tacitus and Dio had to say of her; and sums up: "All which does waygh the more to her true prayse, in coming from the mouthes of Romanes and enemies."

Jonson appreciated that the original versions derived from hostile propagandists. Although a minor point, this deserves notice.

After the masque, Boadicea appeared in straight theatre. Unfortunately Shakespeare did not write about her. His plays come within a generation and a neighbouring tribe of hers in *Cymbeline* who was, historically, the early first century monarch of south-east Britain, his capital at Colchester—Camulodunum, the first city which Boadicea sacked.

In Shakespeare's lifetime John Fletcher wrote *Bonduca,* which was performed in 1610 by the Shakespearian Kings Men with Richard Burbage in the lead. Either because Burbage had to have the chief part or because after the long reign of Elizabeth the public had had enough of female rule, Boadicea is not the most important character in this play. Burbage's

Cataract dominates. He is the quintessence of self-righteous masculine virtue. He commands the army of his cousin, the queen, and reacts in the most superior manner to all her noble utterances, telling her to "go spin." When the younger daughter lures the Roman who is in love with her into a trap which she has baited with herself, Cataract appears, tells her that sort of thing isn't done, and sets the trusting Roman free.

Boadicea is allowed to die nobly, proclaiming:

> If you would keep your laws and Empire whole
> Place in your Roman flesh a British soul.

But Cataract gets the final curtain, Suetonius ordering:

> March on, and through the camp, on every tongue
> The virtues of great Cataract be sung.

The plot has only a very vague similarity with the Tacitean narrative.

There were two other plays about Boadicea, by Richard Hopkins in 1697 and by Richard Glover in 1753. In the second of these Garrick took the part of Dumatrix, who is the commander of her army in this version; for once again she is not allowed to lead herself. She dies off stage, "blind with despair and disappointed fury." It seems that her brief phase of popularity is over.

4. The Roman conquest of Britain after 43 A.D. was a prelude to Boadicea's revolt in 60 A.D. Here Caractacus, leader of the British, appears before the Emperor Claudius after his betrayal to the Romans by Queen Cartimandua of the Brigantes.

CARACTACUS BEFORE CLAUDIUS.

5. An imperious Boadicea harangues her almost naked followers in a romantic nineteenth century painting. The legendary Boadicea, so beloved by the British, is always accompanied by her chariot and her two lovely daughters.

6. Here Boadicea has taken on the elaborate costumes of the eighteenth century for a stage presentation of 1778. Apparently the spear alone is enough to signify her role as the British Queen.

But Milton poured the coldest water on her. In his *History of Britain* he wrote: "The truth is that in this battle and whole business the Britons never more plainly manifested themselves to be right barbarians: no rules, no foresight, no forecast, experience, or estimation, either of themselves or of their enemies: such confusion, such impotence, as seemed likest not to a war, but to the wild hurry of a distracted woman, with as mad a crew at her heels."

Poor Boadicea, her reputation had never sunk so low! But what she suffered from one poet writing prose was redeemed by another writing verse. In 1782 Cowper published his Ode. In this he introduces a Druid prophesying future greatness. A shrewd stroke, that! The queen might lose the war but her race would inherit the earth—as the British were busily doing at that time. And ten thousand read it for every one who read Milton's *History*. The legend received the kiss of life.

> When the British warrior queen,
> > Bleeding from the Roman rods,
> Sought, with an indignant mien,
> > Counsel of her country's gods.
>
> Sage beneath a spreading oak
> > Sat the Druid, hoary chief;

Ev'ry burning word he spoke
   Full of rage, and full of grief.

***

Rome shall perish—write that word
   In the blood that she has spilt;
Perish, hopeless and abhorr'd,
   Deep in ruin as in guilt.

***

Then the progeny that springs
   From the forests of our land,
Arm'd with thunder, clad with wings,
   Shall a wider world command.

Regions Caesar never knew
   Thy posterity shall sway,
Where his eagles never flew,
   None invincible as they.

Such the bard's prophetic words,
   Pregnant with celestial fire,
Bending, as he swept the chords
   Of his sweet but awful lyre.

She, with all a monarch's pride,
   Felt them in her bosom glow;
Rush'd to battle, fought, and died;
   Dying, hurl'd them at the foe.

Ruffians, pitiless as proud,
   Heav'n awards the vengeance due;
Empire is on us bestow'd,
   Shame and ruin wait for you.

Tennyson also write of Boadicea. But his poem was aimed at a more cultured audience—and is one of the least known of his works. It imitates the difficult metre of Catullus's *Atys*. It begins:

> While about the shore of Mona those Neronian
> legionaries
> Burnt and broke the grove and altar of the Druid and
> Druidess,
> Far in the East Boadicea, standing loftily charioted,
> Mad and maddening all that heard her in her fierce
> volubility,
> Girt by half the tribes of Britain, near the colony
> Camulodune,
> Yell'd and shriek'd between her daughters o'er a wild
> confederacy.

Its middle is prophecy:

> Fear not, isle of blowing woodland, isle of silvery
> parapets,
> Tho' the Roman eagle shadow thee, tho' the gathering
> enemy narrow thee,
> Thou shalt wax and he shall dwindle, thou shalt
> be the mighty one yet!

And it ends with a moral:

> Out of evil evil flourishes, out of tyranny tyranny buds
> Ran the land with Roman slaughter, multitudinous
> agonies.
> Perish'd many a maid and matron, many a valorous
> legionary,
> Fell the colony, city, citadel, London, Verulam,
> Camulodune.

We have covered various ways in which the story was carried on through eighteen hundred years, and the legend built up—history, more or less honest or manipulated, drama, poetry. The most effective of all was sculpture. In 1856 Thomas Thornycroft began work on his statue group, *Boadicea and her Daughters*. It was a brilliant conception, well suited to the current mood. The late Victorians sympathised with Boadicea as the first British woman to stand up for what was right, and as symbolic of the beginnings of our far-flung battle line. They also approved of the Romans as empire builders. They managed to reconcile the two, comparing Boadicea's revolt with the Indian Mutiny—after which the Empire went on stronger than ever.

Thornycroft worked at his statue group for fifteen years. The Prince Consort took warm interest in its progress—lending horses from the royal mews as models. In passing, one may note that these splendid beasts cannot have been much like the Icenian ponies, which were used in pairs to pull chariots because they were not strong enough to carry an armed man; it is also interesting that the German Prince Albert should have been attracted to so essentially a British figure. But our chief interest is in the public reaction. This was where the legend as we know it was born.

In July 1871 the art critic of *The Times* saw the plaster cast in Thornycroft's studio in Wilton Place, and wrote of it with enthusiasm:

Mr. Thornycroft has given us fine statuary before now, but he has done nothing, as he has attempted nothing, so great as this. It is not perfect; it has, indeed, faults which at once strike us, but it is not only without doubt the most successful attempt in historical sculpture of this barren time; but it is an achievement which would do credit to any time and any country. The group is nearly twice the size of life, for the figure of Boadicea measures 10 ft. A car, the body of which is wicker-work and the wheels thick circles of solid wood, is drawn at speed by two unbridled horses rudely belted to the heavy pole. They plunge asunder as they sniff battle in the wind; one would dart forward and the other attempts to hold back. In the car, naked to the waist, crouch the Queen's two daughters, and strain their gaze towards the Roman host. The face of one is full of a proud and eager hope, that of the other freezes with horror. Between them stands Boadicea. She lifts her arms high above her head; her right hand is closed round the shaft of a spear, the left is extended, and the whole gesture is of supreme grandeur. Her face and her entire manner finely convey the impression that she is addressing the multitude of the warriors of her tribe. It is the pause before battle, and borne rapidly along the whole array of her people, she calls upon them to take vengeance once and for all and to destroy these Roman soldiers from off the face of British earth. The speed of the car is shown by the incline forward of the figures, the blowing manes and tails of the horses, and the drapery pressed against the outline of the Queen's body. Her face and attitude are instinct with commanding grandeur; she orders the extinction of her foes; she appeals to her people not in frenzy and tears; in tones heart-stirring and eloquent no doubt, but with more pride than rage in them, and her haughty spirit does not dream of defeat.

Thornycroft died in 1885, before the work was cast in bronze. But his son saw to that, with the help of a public subscription. *Boadicea* was presented to the nation.

Then arose the question of where it should be placed. The first suggestion was the tumulus in Parliament Hill Fields, another Hyde Park Corner, another Kensington Gardens, "on a rocky eminence of moderate height, surrounded by water to keep the spectators at the distance from which it should be viewed." In 1902 it was unveiled on its present site by the River Thames at Westminster. Probably more than anything else the statue established Boadicea as a national figure. And it certainly established the scythed chariot.

Parliament Hill had seemed appropriate because it was a traditional site of Boadicea's tomb. But when this was opened it was found by the Society of Antiquaries to be nothing of the sort. A number of other places have been put forward as the Queen's grave. An eighteenth century suggestion was Stonehenge. But though romantically appropriate, it was difficult to explain the gap of a good many centuries between the construction of the memorial and Boadicea's death. In Essex one traditional grave is the tumulus known as the Barlow Hills, and the claim is made for the Bubberies that the name derives from Boadicea. Harrow Weald also claims her grave.

It will be remembered that Dio said she was given a costly funeral. Very likely whatever remained of the fortune of Prasutagus was buried with her. Until it is found, the legend will remain. If it is found, her personal legend will be all the stronger.

II

THE SCENE

Before starting on the historical account, we need in our mind's eye a picture of this island in the first half of the first century A.D. The topography of the country—its ups and downs—and of course its geology was the same then as now. And the native flora was the same, for the habits of nature do not change in a period equivalent to the life span of three or four great oaks. But a drastic change has taken place in what grew where— because man has increasingly interfered, cutting down and planting, and improving what he planted. What we have to picture is the natural distribution of the vegetation. This varies with different soils, exposures and altitudes. The rough and ready way to arrive at our first impression is to see what finally survives on a patch of land left to itself. Botanists call this the vegetational climax.

In this now crowded island only high land which cannot economically be cultivated or land with a deep top layer of unfertile soil is left more or less to itself. But during the last war and the years directly following it we saw bombed areas where vegetation sprang up and battled for survival according to its own laws; and we have all seen patches which for some reason have been left to themselves for a number of years. The strongest plants, best adapted to the particular soil, take over, ousting any delicate strangers which may have been put there and beating off all comers in the form of naturally scattered seeds. Thus, on a small scale, we have seen the Britain of old when most of the land was not cleared or cultivated because the labourers were unskilled, ill-equipped and very few—so few that one of the hardest imaginative tasks is to appreciate the smallness of the population. Probably in the whole island there were not more than half a million people. Naturally they tilled only the most amenable soils and lived in the areas which suited them best, leaving the remainder— 90 per cent or more of the whole—at its vegetational climax.

That only the most suitable areas were cultivated does not rule out the high lands, meaning in this context land of over 1,000 feet above sea level. The high lands were natural fortresses and suitable for habitation for that specific reason. They were of very great importance in our history. But in this story the only mountainous area we are concerned with is Wales, and with it only incidentally. Our scene is the southern half of England, with most of our interest concentrated on the south-east—East Anglia and to a lesser extent Kent and Sussex. Since there are no mountains here it is soil, drainage and cultivation rather than altitude which tint our picture with varying shades of green.

A major factor which has not significantly changed throughout the whole era of history is that Britain gets too much rain. Without drainage, only absorbent or permeable soils carry away the excess. Chalk, sand and gravel are in that class. So is limestone, but this lies outside our particular area. Untilled clay is almost as watertight as putty, and there is a lot of clay in the south-east. In primitive human terms one can cultivate and live in comparative comfort on permeable soils. On clay one cannot. (A pit dwelling in clay inspires nightmares of rheumatism!) Therefore there must be a few paragraphs here on the geology of the south-east.

Chalk and clay are the chief ingredients. The Geological Map of Great Britain shows a

striking pattern of different colours. The chalk
sprouts like a three-fronded plant from Salisbury Plain. The most northerly frond extends
north-eastwards, to end on the north coast of
Norfolk, though it reappears beyond the Wash
in Lincolnshire. To use names one knows
well, the highest and most significant part of
this frond consists of the Wiltshire Downs and
the Chilterns. As it passes through Cambridge-
shire, Suffolk and Norfolk it is scarcely
elevated.

The middle frond of chalk is narrow, high
and distinct: effectively it is the North Downs
which end on the Kentish coast between
Sandwich and Dover, with an island of chalk
to the northwards between Margate and
Ramsgate.

The southern frond is the South Downs
which end in the lofty cliff of Beachy Head.

North of the most northerly frond are the
clays of Buckinghamshire, Bedfordshire, Cam-
bridgeshire and Lincolnshire. Between the
two upper fronds, covering Greater London
and Essex, is another big area of clay. Between
the bottom two fronds, east of Hampshire,
which is almost all chalk, is yet more clay—in
the area of the Weald of Sussex.

So the geological map shows us (ignoring

lesser formations) three fronds of permeable chalk interspersed by heavy, moisture-holding soils. But unfortunately for early man—and perhaps for modern man as well!—that is not quite the surface picture. The geological map shows the basic geology, not the superficial deposits. And the glaciers of the Ice Age deposited a lot of heavy clay on the low ground of East Anglia. The surface chalk was there reduced to a thin band lying up against the marshes of the Fens, which before drainage were uninhabitable except on the islands. Most of the rest is covered with boulder clay. Only in the north-east corner, and in a fringe round the rest of the coast, are there lighter soils, gravel and sand subsoils.

Considering this geological picture, one is not surprised to learn that Salisbury Plain was the cradle of corporate life in this country. Migrants arrived from Brittany and Iberia, and settled on Salisbury Plain. From there they radiated along the fronds of chalk. Thus some reached East Anglia, though Norfolk, Suffolk and Essex received most of their immigrants by sea from northern Europe. But it was on the chalk that the first roads were trodden out. As every walker knows, the Ridgeway, Icknield Way, Pilgrim's Way follow these fronds on dry and springy turf above the sticky clays. On the chalk are the White Horses and the "Roman" camps—many of them much older than the Romans.

The clay land was dangerous if not impenetrable. Anyone who lives on clay, or heavy loam which is clay well charged with decayed vegetable matter, notes that the natural vegetation is forest. The elm with its extensive and flat root system throws out a jungle of suckers which help to anchor it to the ground—and grow into trees themselves. In summer its seeds fall thick as snowflakes in a storm, and its seedlings are wonderfully persistent. The oak is scarcely less prolific. Elders, thorns and briars sprout between. All these grow up and shut off the light from lesser vegetation. The gardener or farmer can easily picture what he would wake to if he fell asleep for twenty years, let alone two thousand. So the lower levels of this island were almost entirely covered by forest.

About three quarters of East Anglia was bordered by sea or by the Fens. To the southwest lay the marshy Thames valley. (All slow-flowing rivers had wide fringes of marsh.) The only easy land approach was by the narrow frond of chalk which had remained upon the surface after the Ice Age. East Anglia might be considered a peninsula within an island. As such we will try to picture it in more detail.

Much of it was clay or heavy loam and had therefore remained in its natural state, although men had for centuries possessed iron instruments capable of cutting down trees. Only farmers were going to alter the vegetational pattern, and farmers have been inclined to do work that is not rewarding. It was no good felling and burning the forest until they had some means of cultivating the clay or heavy loam surface. The primitive plough could not do that.

The primitive plough was derived from a hooked stick used as a hoe. Someone had the excellent idea that instead of pulling this scraper through the earth himself he should arrange for an ox or horse to pull a larger instrument while he steered it from behind. But this did not turn the soil over. It merely left a furrow, as a pig's snout does when it rootles. ("Furrow" and "farrow" both derive from the Old English word for a pig.) This primitive plough—called by the Romans *aratrum* and by the Scandinavians *ard*—is still used in certain parts of the world where the soil

37

is light and dry. In such conditions it leaves a fine tilth suitable for seed, particularly if the ploughing is done twice—first down and then across. That is why the early Celtic fields were roughly square, as we know from air photographs that they were. The pattern is still in some areas discernible.

The scratch method of ploughing is impracticable on clay. There the point merely sticks in, and the harder the pull and push the deeper it sticks. Until there was a more efficient plough the only way of preparing such soil for crops was by the primitive hand method, still employed by gardeners. But digging can only have been practiced on a small scale.

Until quite recently it was believed that a more efficient plough only appeared in Britain with the Anglo-Saxons, well after our period. But now there is strong evidence that the Belgae possessed a heavy metal-shod plough so designed that, with more animals pulling, it could not only cut through clay but turn it over.

The Belgae, probably of German origin, had come to England over the North Sea, first as raiders and then as settlers. One tribe, the Atrebates, settled in the Silchester area of

Hampshire, and another, the Catuvellauni, around the present St. Albans in Hertfordshire. A third tribe, the Trinovantes, occupied Essex. The two latter tribes were thus neighbours of the Iceni of Norfolk and Suffolk. They began to cultivate the clay and heavy loam. This not only provided a bigger farming area but also better crops, for chalk soil is not particularly fertile. Their ploughing method was naturally copied by their neighbours.

Thus the south-east of Britain, ahead of the rest of the island, ahead of most of Europe including the country of the Romans, had achieved a break-through in a double sense. Its people were on the way to prove that agriculture could do more than supply the basic needs of man, that it could make him rich if intelligently practiced. It was making East Anglia—although lacking minerals—richer than neighbouring districts. Its corn and hides were in demand on the continent. Its balance of payments, already on the right side in spite of an increasing demand for luxuries, was constantly improving.

The botanist-archaeologists have even identified the seeds which were sown. Lord Ernle listed them as follows in *English Farming Past and Present*. The wheats were Emmer *(Triticum diococcum)*, Spelt *(T. spelta)* and Broadwheat *(T. vulgare)*. The barley was Bere *(Hordeum vulgare)*. The oats were *Avena strigosa* and *A. brevis*. The bean was the pea-sized *Vicia fabia*.

The detective-like techniques employed to discover secrets of the past are fascinating. The close study of pollen is an excellent example. Pollen, the minute male element of plants which nature throws abroad with her usual profligacy—and few grains of which find a chance of fulfilling their function of fertilising the ovule—possesses a skin which is practically indestructible—except when in close contact with its female counterpart. In its bachelor state the skin, the exine, remains intact for tens or hundreds of years, for thousands in bogland. And the exine of every species is characteristically marked. Thus it is possible to determine under the microscope what plants formerly grew in the place where the pollen grains are found. More than that, one can know (calling in another science) when they grew. Still more than that, by taking out a cubic unit of soil from a fixed depth one can identify and proportion the various species. A paper entitled *Pollen-Analytic Evidence for the Cultivation of Cannabis in England,* kindly provided by its

7. An early nineteenth view of Boadicea leading her followers.

8. The Desborough mirror, a triumph of British craftsmanship, shows on its back the swirling designs of Celtic art. Dating from the first century A.D., it might have been used by Boadicea herself had she been at all concerned about her appearance.

10. Bronze head of the Emperor Claudius, found in the river Alde at Saxmundham, Suffolk, some forty miles from Colchester. There is little doubt that it was part of an equestrian statue in the Temple of Claudius at Colchester, and was torn off and carried away by Boadicea's troops when they butchered the last defenders of Colchester in the Temple.

author, Dr. H. Godwin of Cambridge, begins: "A detailed pollen diagram from an East Anglian Lake, Old Buckenham Mere, registers vegetational changes from late Glacial times to the present. When a chronology is projected upon it this allows the reconstruction of the effects of historic and prehistoric man upon local vegetation through the last 5,000 years."

This is not quoted to suggest that Boadicea's people took drugs! In fact cannabis was not grown in any quantity before Anglo-Saxon times. But it helps the layman to accept that even the most detailed statements about the first century may have adequate scientific backing.

By no means all the open ground was tilled. Most of it was pasture. The margins of the Fens provided excellent grazing. Our ancestors bred cattle, similar to the present Highland Cattle of Scotland, also pigs, goats, sheep, horses, fowls—a variety of domestic animals almost as wide as now, though the goose was treated as a semi-sacred pet and not eaten before the Romans came. The edible snail was a Roman importation, which never became a popular form of diet. This island was, apparently, already conservative in its tastes.

A pleasant incident about a Roman snail may

perhaps be interpolated. In *Thirteen Rivers to the Thames* Brian Waters tells of the finding of one (they are large, round, white and unmistakeable) within an hour's walk of the Roman villa at Chedworth. It and its ancestors had taken at least fifteen hundred years to cover three miles.

On food of their own choosing and production the inhabitants of first century East Anglia lived well. Their skeletons show them to have been a sturdy people, nearly as tall as the present average. They ground their grain by hand and baked bread. Having pottery they could cook by other means besides roasting and grilling. Since the scythe had come with the iron age they could cut hay to keep their beasts alive in the winter. And of course they could make weapons. They needed weapons, not only against human enemies. With forest surrounding the farmsteads and settlements, prowling wolves, bears and foxes would take toll of the farm animals— though the British lion is only heraldic, and of later date at that. But the forest also supplied game to supplement the food supply.

The people used a currency on the Roman pattern. Some of the developments and comforts of Roman civilization came by the hands of traders from the continent before the Roman conquest. Clothing was of wool and perhaps linen too, coloured with vegetable dyes. (We are still to describe Boadicea's striking costume.) Gold ornaments were worn. Continental wine was drunk as well as the native barley beer.

The settlements were small and scattered. The idea of a large centre of population, containing law courts, market and theatre, was a Roman importation. The houses were huts of the simplest design and of perishable materials, wood and thatch. Stone could only be used when suitable stone was easily available, and there is none in East Anglia. Bricks were scarcely if at all used before the Roman invasion. But living conditions, at least for the better-off members of the community, were probably almost as comfortable as in the early Middle Ages. Wattle and daub was already being used—these words are written in an East Anglian thatched cottage, partly built of wattle and daub—so there is a link even with a still existing type of building!

Finds of highly decorated weapons, shields and armour, and also of gold ornaments, have helped to build up a picture of an aristocracy

as well as a peasant class. The chiefs were
gorgeously arrayed. They wore armour in
battle, and helmets richly embossed and
decorated with the effigies of animal heads,
which it has been suggested anticipated the
medieval crest. In fact the tribal warfare was
already tending towards that of the days of
chivalry. One champion would call out
another from the enemy ranks to settle the issue
by single combat while their hosts stood
watching. This form of spectator warfare
suited the peasant who went into battle half
naked, perhaps painted with woad as Caesar
said, but armed and protected by nothing
better than blunt-pointed slashing sword and
wicker shield.

Chariot fighting was a speciality. This
preceded the use of cavalry, because the lively
little horses were not strong enough to carry
an armoured man. The tactics of chariot
warfare will be described later. But a negative
discovery about the chariots themselves must
be admitted at once. Not one with scythes on
the axles has been found in England.

They may have been tried (Tacitus does
mention them as once used in Caledonia), but
a moment of thought untinged by romance
will show that they would soon be discarded

11. A limestone head from Boadicea's time is strongly Celtic in feeling, but yet betrays the inescapable influence of Roman art in the treatment of the hair.

12 -13. An actual British chariot, reconstructed from remains found on Anglesey, contrasts sharply with the lumbering bathtubs in which Boadicea has traditionally been portrayed. The British bits, decorated with Celtic art, are the type that would have been used with Boadicea's chariots.

14 -15.   Coins of the Iceni, Boadicea's tribe, depict horses, and a wolf (upper left). Boadicea would have known such coins, which were certainly in use until the Romans came in 43 A.D. The British ploughman with his oxen, dating from Roman times, was found near Durham.

Found at Pierce Bridge
Co Durham.

W.B.SCOTT,   GIVEN BY

16-17. This bronze boss, or centre (above), of a British shield with its swirling Celtic decoration was raised from the Thames at Battersea. It dates from the early first century A.D. and is the type that Boadicea's troops would have used against the Romans. The golden torque (below), from the first century B.C., may have been worn by a priest, or by a ruler like Boadicea.

as impracticable. They would cause havoc in the enemy ranks. But at some stage of the battle the charioteers would have to return to their own ranks—where they would cause similar havoc. A Celtic chariot has been reconstructed from fragments found in Anglesey. Lightness is the guiding principle of its design, for the vehicle had to bump and bounce over the most uneven ground. The Anglesey chariot consists of two strong wheels, a long axle with a yoke for the harnessing of two horses, and an open wooden framework for the driver to stand on, partly protected by wicker sides. It is about as different as it could be from the chariot in the statue group at Westminster in memory of Boadicea. This may be sad but it is true.

Of things which are not material, and which therefore cannot literally be dug up—social behaviour and organization, for instance—we know much less. There were no native records whatever until after the Romans had left. All that we have are Latin inscriptions and Roman memorial sculptures. Certainly the Romans, with Julius Caesar well to the fore, described some of the native customs. But one cannot help suspecting propaganda or inadequate knowledge. For instance, Caesar speaks of the

Britons of his day having their wives in common—an arrangement which strikes one as still more impractical than having scythes on chariot wheels.

It is almost certainly impossible to get at the whole truth as regards social structure and habits. An ignominious attempt is made by M. E. Seebohm in *The Evolution of the English Farm*. She summarises the Celtic tribal laws and customs as set down by Howell Da in the tenth century in Wales. Admittedly this is some nine hundred years after our period. But the conservatism of mountain people, particularly those of Wales, has been proved whenever a point is provable, and it is at least probable that these laws and customs were based on a much more ancient Celtic structure.

The law regarding the status and independence of a wife certainly deserves mention for its direct bearing on this story. She was entitled to leave her husband before the end of the seventh year of her marriage, taking her share of the household goods, children and stock with her. This remarkably long probationary period might well account for Caesar's remark about wives being held in common. And the evident high standing of women among the Celts helps to explain why

Boadicea was accepted as the leader of the rebellion.

Let us stand back from the easel to look appraisingly at the picture we have been painting of first century East Anglia. The convex eastern side of this bow-shaped projection of the British island thrusts forward towards the north coast of Europe. It is in effect a peninsula, largely surrounded by sea or marshland, and further protected by forest except along a thin causeway of chalk. Within itself it was largely forested, and by this forest divided into north and south—except along the thin line of surface chalk. In the southern half lived the Belgic tribes, the Catuvellauni and Trinovantes. In the north, principally in Norfolk, lived the Iceni. They were of mixed ancestry but had no Belgic blood.

The two halves quarrelled, threw up fortifications between each other across the only practicable line of advance. Most of the earthworks which remain are of later date, but at least one—at Wandlebury near Cambridge—belongs to this period.

The Belgic tribes had felt the weight of Julius Caesar's hand in the middle of the preceding century. The Iceni were beyond its reach. When nearly a hundred years had passed without a return of the Romans they may well have felt that they would never come back. We can be sure at least that the Iceni were more concerned about the ambitions of their Belgic neighbours, whose swords were as good as their ploughshares, than they were of distant Rome. And meanwhile they profited by the ever increasing trade with the continent.

The poorer class lived a hard but not under-nourished life. The farmers had the power to increase their holdings. The artisans and craftsmen—tool-makers, armourers, black-smiths, carpenters, cloth-makers, jewellers—found an ample market for their goods. The aristocracy lived a life of barbaric splendour, eating and drinking well, uncultured and uninhibited, stimulated by such fighting as there was much as they were stimulated by hunting. One cannot suggest that there was a national spirit, but the people enjoyed their way of life and had no fear that it would ever be upset.

III

THE ROMAN INVASION

We must now look at Britain through Roman eyes, first those of Julius Caesar, then of his successors; for the climax of this story is an explosion, and we must know all the ingredients.

Caesar said he crossed the channel in 55 B.C. because the Belgae in Britain were aiding, morally or materially, their kinsmen in northern Gaul, with whom he was directly engaged. No doubt this was a main reason (he had crossed the Rhine with a similar purpose) but it was not the only one. Caesar was ambitious, and even a partial conquest of the British island would add enormously to his prestige. Therefore he took the greatest risk of his adventurous career.

We now think of ourselves as an island race, different from the rest of the world. The geographers of the early civilizations, Greek and Roman, considered Britain as monstrously different. Their world was bounded by seas of which the ocean which lapped the European continent was part. Britain was outside the mass of land; therefore it was another world, an excrescence which ought not to be there. It was *alter orbis*. Ancients of the mental level of those who now read science fiction peopled Britain with creatures quite as strange as our modern Martians.

It was a magic island, favoured by the Gods— probably because it was the homeland of the Druids. But also it was a rich island. Merchant adventurers had been there and brought back gold and other metals, including silver which was always needed by Rome for her coinage; also hides, clever hunting dogs, and handsome slaves, the produce of tribal wars.

Caesar gathered together all the Gallic merchants who had traded with Britain, and questioned them. They would tell him nothing. But he knew the Belgae, close relatives of the British Belgae; and he had probably seen Britons in Gaul. They were fairer and taller than the Romans, but they were men like other men. They might be conquered. He sent a ship to examine the coast, for he rightly anticipated that the greatest danger lay in crossing the Channel— the Ocean, as he called it.

He crossed with two legions in seventy ships, which included warships as well as transports. He faced an opposed landing, and the water was too shallow for his ships to reach the shore. The legionaries, brave as they were under conditions which they knew, hesitated to disembark until the standard bearer of the X Legion jumped into the water, calling out, "Leap down, men, unless you want to abandon the Eagle to the enemy...." This is another incident remembered from school days, though not by so many as those who learned the name of Boadicea: national pride plays its part. Once the well-drilled legions had drawn up in tight formation on the shore—a solid line of shields from which there darted out the short, sharp stabbing swords—they soon had the ascendancy. The British attacked bravely, wildly, swinging their longer swords, which failed in effect against the Roman armour. Their own magic protection of woad was not effective. They withdrew.

Caesar could not follow because the ships which carried his cavalry had been driven back by contrary winds. Another storm wrecked or damaged a number of his transports at anchor. In spite of his initial success he was in a weak position. In these circumstances he could hope for little, and he achieved nothing of military significance—unless one considers the operation only as a reconnaissance. He was fortunate to get his forces back to Gaul before the October storms.

He was much more successful in the following year with a force of no less than five legions and auxiliaries—28,000 infantry and 2,000 cavalry. Faced by Cassivellaunus, who led the mixed army of British tribes, he forced his way first across the River Stour and then across the Thames.

The British, having been beaten in pitched battle, continued to oppose the Romans by guerilla tactics. But Caesar, helped by the Trinovantes, managed to find, capture and destroy the stronghold of Cassivellaunus. This was, it appears certain, the earthworks still to be seen at Wheathampstead, near St. Albans (the Roman Verulamium). Cassivellaunus escaped, to continue his guerilla tactics while Romans remained on British soil. But Caesar had achieved enough to justify his second expedition. He had won the allegiance of the Trinovantes, enemies of the Catuvellauni. He had been in a position to demand hostages and tribute—though whether he ever received either is far from certain. He withdrew to Gaul after a brilliant campaign.

It is tempting to wonder what would have

happened if he had returned again, or if any Roman commander had launched an invasion while the ruthless efficiency of the legions was still within living memory. But almost a century was to pass before a Roman soldier again stood on British soil. Memories of discomfiture are short, particularly when there are no written records, so the British tribes remembered only that Caesar had twice been forced to withdraw. As for Rome, she was occupied elsewhere.

Caesar's attention was fully engaged during his last ten years, first by revolt in Gaul and then by all that followed his crossing of the Rubicon. Augustus, the first Emperor, who inherited from the man who was assassinated from fear that he might declare himself Emperor, spent his long reign in consolidation. He made no attempts at invasion. Tiberius also left Britain alone. The mad Caligula assembled an invading force in the Channel ports about Boulogne. It never sailed. What exactly happened is obscure, but the legions refused to embark and were withdrawn.

So the invasion was delayed until 43 A.D., when Claudius saw his opportunity. The most thorough preparations were made, not only military but political, for it had always been the

53

Roman way to divide their adversaries, seeking allies by bribes and promises. Thus at least the Trinovantes, who had submitted to Caesar, had been kept friendly. Certain princes, ousted by their rivals, had fled to Rome—where they were put to good use.

The invasion coincided, no doubt intentionally, with a critical phase in the leadership of the powerful Belgic tribes whose hatred of the Romans had not faded in three generations. Their rule and influence stretched from their capital of Colchester up to Newmarket, where they bordered the Iceni, through Northamptonshire and the Cotswolds and down to the south coast. In 40 A.D. their king, Cunobelinus, died; and the Belgic realm was divided between his sons. Togodumnus inherited the eastern part, and Caractacus the south and west. The Romans evidently hoped to drive a diplomatic wedge between these two. But they failed. Whatever the individual ambitions of the brothers may have been, they were united in their hostility to Rome.

The feelings of the other tribes were different. They tended to prefer the devil they did not know. The people of Kent, afraid of complete absorption by the aggressive, imperialistic Belgae, welcomed Roman intervention. The

Iceni did not go as far as that, and did not in any case expect to be occupied by Roman soldiers, as Kent was bound to be. But they were under continual pressure from the Belgae to their south, and had recently lost to them their outpost fortifications on the Gog and Magog hills near Cambridge. They needed help.

Their king played his hand with care. We cannot be certain that Prasutagus, husband of Boadicea, was already king; but the Icenian ruler of the day behaved with a caution which fits the character of Prasutagus. He was ready to acknowledge a greater invader, to pay lip service and even tribute, if his kingdom was guaranteed against further incursions by the native enemy. Prasutagus was a rich man, primarily concerned with the conservation of his wealth and the peaceful development of Icenia.

It must have been clear enough that invasion was intended. One does not have to go far out into the Straits of Dover to see the coast of France, and from very early in the year 43 there had been a great deal of activity there. Ships were built or modified, and concentrated at Boulogne. Stores poured in by the waggon load and were piled up ready for loading.

Some 40,000 troops and a large number of horses were collected in camps. Preparations on such a scale must have been evident to fishermen. And the Gallic merchants, who since Caesar's day had been coming to Britain in increasing numbers, would carry detailed accounts. It was abundantly clear that the Romans meant to cross the Straits.

But week after week went by, and still they did not come. Something had evidently gone wrong. It began to look as if once again the invasion had been called off.

The soldiers were unwilling to cross the "Ocean." They were part of the proudest, best-trained and disciplined army in the world; but they were superstitious, and they had heard stories about this island outside the world. Some years before, a part of the army of Germanicus had been embarked from the mouth of the River Ems for winter quarters further south. It should have been a short and easy passage, but a storm blew up.

"The Atlantic is the stormiest of all the seas..." wrote Tacitus, who was not generally given to exaggeration. "Here, then, was disaster on a new and unprecedented scale. On the one side were the shores of enemy country, on the other seas so wide and deep that this is thought to be the last, landless ocean. Some of the ships were sunk: more were cast away in far, uninhabited islands, where the troops either starved to death or ate the bodies of the horses washed up with them... Some had even been driven ashore in Britain, and were sent back by the petty kings of the island. As they came in from their far adventures they had marvels to tell: fearful hurricanes, strange birds, strange monsters, half human, half animal. All these they had seen or imagined in their fears."

It is interesting that the "petty kings" of eastern Britain were careful to avoid any cause of quarrel with the Romans. They sent back the castaways. But the stories of the soldiers who were returned would lose nothing with each re-telling, and they must have been told a hundred times. The troops of Caligula had set a precedent by refusing to sail. This was repeated.

The military commander, Aulus Plautius, was at a double disadvantage. Sound general though he was, he lacked the spark of personality which inspires men beyond reason, out of reason. And he was unknown to three of the four legions which had been placed under his command. He shrank from disciplining the mutineers, and sent to Rome for help and guidance.

Narcissus, a freed man, a Greek ex-slave who by quickness of mind had achieved high office, was sent from Rome. At first he offered himself as a butt to the soldiers, allowing them to let off steam. Then he talked them round. They embarked without further protest. All this must have occupied about two months, and the campaigning season was short.

Aulus Plautius may not have been an inspiring general, but he was a lucky one. He carried his army over to Richborough, between Ramsgate and Deal, where he made an unopposed landing. The British force which had been waiting for him—not a regular army in any sense but a force made up of chiefs and their retainers, farmers and the like—had broken up and gone home. It must have seemed to them that this was another false alarm.

That was Plautius's first piece of good fortune. The potentially dangerous landing on a hostile coast was achieved without loss in the landlocked roadstead of Wantsun Channel, which was then navigable. This success paid a dividend, for the soldiers who had successfully overcome their fears were enormously pleased with themselves. Morale could not have been higher. The Roman plan included diversions and decoy landings. But this did not prove necessary.

In our knowledge of the invasion we are much poorer than we might be because the relevant books of Tacitus have been lost. But the details at this stage matter little to this story. The Roman advance, wonderfully efficient, brave, and ingenious in overcoming obstacles had to proceed a long way before the Iceni were pricked by it. It may be described briefly. It almost appears a game of chess with the pieces of one side moving systematically, logically, almost safely across the board until they had reached the half-way line.

The British forces quickly regathered under Caractacus and Togodumnus. The defenders were superior in numbers to the invaders, but that was their only advantage. While the Romans were perfectly co-ordinated and trained as a whole, the British were a collection of units under individual leaders—wild, brave men, trying to outdo each other. But as the Romans never forgave a defeat, they never forgot a lesson; and in one part or another of their vast Empire they had always been fighting. Therefore they had moved with the times in warfare.

The British tribes had not. For almost a century they had only experienced squabbles with their neighbours, and had not progressed at all in the continental sense. They still practiced the same chariot tactics which Caesar had noted with professional interest:

"Chariots are used in action in the following way. First of all the charioteers drive all over the field, the warriors hurling javelins; and generally they throw the enemy's ranks into confusion by the terror inspired by their horses and the clatter of their wheels. Then, having driven between the ranks of their own cavalry, the warriors jump off their chariots and fight on foot. The drivers meanwhile gradually withdraw from the action and range the chariots in such a position that, if the warriors are hard-pressed by the enemy, they may easily get back to their vehicles. Thus they combine the mobility of cavalry and the steadiness of infantry. And they become so efficient from constant practice and training that they will drive their horses at full gallop, keeping them well in hand, down a steep slope, check and turn them in an instant, run along the shaft (between the horses) and skip back again into the chariot with the greatest nimbleness."

Such circus-skilful tactics must have been hypnotising, terrifying to an enemy—at first. But once the novelty had gone they could not succeed against a Roman unit moving as an armoured mass. They could not win a pitched battle.

A pitched battle was fought on the Medway. Plautius had under his command troops highly trained and experienced in river crossings. These swam over fully armed and succeeded in holding the bridgehead thus formed. They reduced the charioteers to lightly-equipped infantry by killing their horses. While this fighting was going on Vespasian, the future emperor, got another force across unopposed in a different place. Presumably with boats or a pontoon bridge he quickly built up his strength on the further bank. So the first day of the battle ended. Next morning the Britons renewed their assaults on the bridgehead, but the Romans, who had no doubt used the dark hours to reinforce their position, were strong enough to hold their ground, and by evening they had consolidated. They drove the British tribal units into the woods.

This was the crucial battle. The Thames at low tide proved a lesser obstacle. The Romans even managed to capture a bridge intact, which

61

suggests that the British forces were thoroughly disorganised. Togodumnus had been killed. Caractacus withdrew to the west. No other serious resistance could be expected on the way to the Belgic capital at Colchester.

The campaign so far had been swift and ruthlessly efficient. But on the borders of Essex it was checked for many weeks. For the Emperor had to come all the way from Rome to lead the final advance, and although a messenger using relays of horses could cover the thousand miles in a fortnight, an imperial suite was much slower. Dio tells us that Claudius brought elephants. If so it dates the first appearance of these animals in Britain. One cannot help wondering how they were got across the Channel.

This halt by Plautius was tactful, not tactical. It allowed Caractacus to get clear away. The Roman commander and Governor-designate of the Province of Britain may not at the time have realized that this mattered. For what could Caractacus do in the wild and mountainous lands of the west after his own Belgic forces had been so thoroughly routed?

He could have achieved nothing—except for the Druids. The Druids were implacably opposed to Rome as were the Jews. They may be likened to the Jews in that their cult knew no frontier. They were the only unifying power among the Celts, in both Gaul and Britain. They provided, too, the tutors for the youth of all the aristocratic families. Thus their influence was both subtle and profound.

The Druids saw in Caractacus a leader who could be counted upon to oppose the Roman domination. With their backing he was accepted as war leader by the Silures and Ordovices of southern and central Wales. Here where Druid influence was strongest, where the country was difficult to penetrate and the people most stubborn in their opposition, a centre of resistance built up which endured until the time of Boadicea's rebellion, and in fact was then of crucial importance.

But to return to the late summer of 43 A.D., Claudius came from Rome, fought a battle with the people of Essex, and led the victorious entry into Colchester. There he made treaties with the various tribes, and returned to Rome for his triumph. What remains of the dedicatory inscription on the Arch of Claudius states that "eleven kings of the Britons" submitted to him. Professor Donald Dudley says wittily that no British XI is harder to pick, but it is at least possible that Prasutagus was one. It would have fitted with his cautious and conciliatory policy. In any case the Iceni were for the moment left alone.

Aulus Plautius, following this first stage of the invasion, appears to have been instructed to establish a viable Roman province as quickly as possible. The first necessity was to make it secure. Vespasian was ordered to sweep westwards along the south coast of the island. This he did, finding it necessary to reduce a whole series of hill forts, Maiden Castle among them. Plautius himself established Colchester as his base, then cautiously explored in a north-westerly direction. He recognized the line of the Fosse Way as the best natural frontier he could hope to find. Though far from impregnable, it ran north-eastwards, parallel to the Bristol Channel and the River Avon. It continued along the limestone escarpment which limits the Cotswolds, looking down into the thickly forested country to the northward. It continued through Leicester to Lincoln— though thereabouts in less defensible terrain. The River Trent helped to seal off the eastern end. He did not aim to make this a fixed defensive line, like that which Hadrian later built between the Solway and the Tyne.

Instead, the Fosse Way was the axis of a belt of fortified encampments some thirty miles in depth.

When Plautius relinquished his appointment in 47 A.D. he considered that the south-eastern corner of Britain was effectively under Roman control.

Ostorius Scapula took over the governorship in the autumn, as the legions were going into winter quarters. Caractacus chose that moment to strike. He had spent the last four years establishing his military leadership in Wales, and in indoctrinating his followers with hatred of the Romans. He had first-hand experience of their cruelties, but the surest threat to rouse the independent Welsh was that of slavery. The Romans needed slaves to work the mines. They fought to gather prisoners for this purpose.

The Silures crossed the Severn and drove deep into the province between the Fosse Way forts, shattering the *pax Romana* and waking among the subject people memories of ancient freedom. The new governor had to take the legions out of winter quarters and drive Caractacus back into Wales.

That was only a beginning, to tide over the winter months. Caractacus could not be left to attack again at will and at any point of his own choosing along the Fosse Way frontier. Therefore Scapula decided to hunt him down by launching a many-pronged advance into Wales, along the coast and up the valleys.

There was a major objection to this typically thorough Roman plan. Scapula lacked sufficient reserves to maintain his garrisons in East Anglia and at the same time to invade Wales. He got round this by establishing a colony for old soldiers in the Colchester area. These men were retired from active service but by no means too old to fight in an emergency. There was the disadvantage that the *colonia* could only be created by expropriating land, which naturally alienated the native owners. But the old soldiers released garrison troops for the Welsh campaign.

Scapula took another gamble also. He ordered that the eastern tribes should be disarmed. The weapons and armour of the Celts were, as we have said, heirlooms passed down from father to son. They were not things that a man of spirit was prepared to part with. Added to this, disarmament involved search, aggressive intrusion into the home. The Iceni rose in revolt. This was evidently a burst of anger, an unplanned uprising. It was quickly suppressed. So sure was Scapula of the effectiveness of this suppression that he left Prasutagus on the throne.

With his full force in the field, Scapula encircled Caractacus. The Celtic chief moved northwards through the high country of the Ordovici, but was headed off. At last in a steep and narrow place he turned at bay. After a day of hard fighting the Romans were the victors, but when they counted the dead Caractacus was not among them.

He had escaped to the north across the line between the Mersey and the Humber where the extensive territory of Brigantes began. But he had chosen badly. The Queen's party of the Brigantes was pro-Roman, and Queen Carti-mandua handed over Caractacus to Scapula in chains.

If the Governor believed that the Welsh question was thereby settled he was quickly undeceived. The Silures were made only more obstinate and troublesome by this defeat and treachery. Avoiding pitched battles, they kept up a continuous series of raids, skirmishes and ambushes. Harassed by this elusive enemy, Scapula's health broke down, and he died.

During the long governorship of Didius Gallus, which followed, the situation in Britain did not materially change. But it changed in Rome. Nero became emperor at the age of seventeen. At first, while still swayed by his tutor, Seneca, and by Burrhus, prefect of the Praetorian Guards, his policy was moderate and cautious. He saw Britain as an investment which had paid no dividends. Trouble in the west had prevented the exploitation of tin and silver mines, while the expense of patrolling the frontier remained as high as ever in lives and money. The province came near to being written off as uneconomic.

But by the year 57 Nero felt strong enough to ignore his advisers, and began to decide policy in his own wilful way. Britain must be *made* to pay. The reasons why it had not yet done so could be summed up by the single word, Wales. Therefore, Nero decided, the Welsh question must be settled once and for all.

The man chosen by the Emperor to implement this decision was Quintus Veranius. He was a man in the prime of life, with a reputation for initiative and drive. He stated confidently that he would conquer the whole of Britain within two years.

The British climate killed him in one.

IV

THE CONQUEST
OF WALES

Nero could not abide being thwarted by God
or man. But it took a long time for the new
Governor of an outpost of the Empire to take
up his appointment, particularly if his pred-
ecessor had not been relieved of his post in
the ordinary course of routine but had died
unexpectedly. First, news of the death had to
be carried to Rome. The letter sent by messenger
relay from Britain might take two weeks to
cross the Channel with its often unfavourable
winds, be carried to Marseilles and thence on
by ship to the capital. The land route round the
head of the Ligurian Sea and down half the
length of the Peninsula could scarcely be
quicker, and in the early stages would be
dangerous.

In Rome, when the successor had been
agreed upon, it would be necessary to recall him
from wherever he was serving. With an
empire which virtually surrounded the Mediterranean and covered Europe as far east as
Germany, the man selected might have to be

brought from a thousand miles away. Having been given his appointment, he required thorough briefing by the various departments of state before he was ready to leave. The Governor was primarily a military man. He was responsible for the frontiers of his province and for the maintenance of law and order within them, the army being directly under his command. Many matters—customs dues, the collection of taxes and so on were the concern of the Procurator, the senior Treasury official. But the Governor was finally responsible if anything went wrong. He needed to master a great deal of information on his province. And then he had to travel there with his staff, both military and clerical. He could not hope to take up his appointment in less than three or four months.

The new Governor, Suetonius Paulinus, reached Britain in the autumn of 58. He was essentially a man of action, which was why he had been chosen.

Some fifteen years earlier he had been Governor of Mauritania, roughly corresponding with Morocco and Algeria. The Mauritanians were wild hillmen who attacked from their fortresses in the Atlas mountains and could never be pinned down. Suetonius had led his legions over the range and down to the oases beyond from which the tribesmen drew their provisions and reinforcements. There he systematically destroyed the enemy's power to resist. It was a daring and masterly campaign, involving a passage through very difficult country, ideal for ambuscades. By his success he finished in the shortest possible time a war which might well have been indefinitely protracted. In recognition of this he was awarded a triumph and made consul. Thus he had a background of governmental experience. But there can be little doubt that his new appointment was due to his reputation as a dashing general of proved ability in mountain warfare.

There must have been a vast number of administrative questions awaiting decision in a province which had been without a governor for so long. Suetonius did not spend much time on them. He left most to the Procurator, Catus Decianus, whom he had found in office on his arrival. There are many instances in Roman history of trouble between Governor and Procurator. Apart from their different yet interdependent responsibilities, they were almost always of quite different origin. The

Governor was a soldier, a traditionalist, a patrician. The Procurator was a businessman or civil servant. They were most unlikely to get on socially together. They tended to see as little of each other as they possibly could. Suetonius and Catus were not exceptions to this rule.

Suetonius considered the position in military terms. The capital of the province was Colchester, tucked away in the south-east with good sea connections with northern Gaul. It lay in the country of the Trinovantes, a conquered tribe which meekly accepted subjugation. In fact they had co-operated in the process of Romanization. Colchester was being built up—by Trinovantine labour—into a show-piece Roman town. There was a senate house, a theatre, and a temple to Claudius. This last, which was of great significance later, needs explanation. Every Roman emperor automatically became a god when he died. But Claudius decided that, as far as Britain was concerned, he would be considered as divine while still alive. So he commanded the building of a temple to himself when he entered Colchester in triumph in 43 A.D. No doubt he was in euphoric mood, and the Senate in Rome had given their approval in advance to any arrangements that he saw fit to make.

The temple was large and expensively constructed—as one can still see from the excavations—elevated above the surrounding ground and with an altar in front. Apart from the fact that Claudius was still in this world when it was inaugurated, the temple at Colchester was part of the established process of Roman colonisation and integration. We have seen modern dictators insisting on everything short of divine worship. The Romans carried the cult of personality to its logical extreme. They found that this served to unify a province, to give it a focus and a means of expressing proper gratitude for the *pax Romana*.

But maintenance of such a cult cost money, which the Romans themselves had no intention of expending. The Roman idea of worship—of whatever god—demanded the observation of a series of festivals throughout the year. These included not only religious sacrifices but games and musical and literary competitions. These were the responsibility in both time and money of the priests. The priests were members of the local aristocratic families, elected in rotation. Only a few tribes could be involved in the Colchester cult. Therefore the burden of maintenance fell heavily on the few. As Tacitus put it, "in the guise of religion the chosen priests poured out their whole fortunes." And for those who were not priests, the temple to Claudius remained a symbol of Roman conquest.

The patient Trinovantes had another burden put upon them—the provision of agricultural land for veteran legionaries living in Colchester. These tough old soldiers soon had the former owners working for them as slaves. And they constantly increased their holdings by grabbing more land. This was outside the law, but the Governor turned a blind eye to it because they could be relied upon to keep the local people quiet.

Besides Colchester, there was the newly-born and rapidly growing business town of London. This was inhabited by merchants and their families and did brisk trade with the continent. Twenty miles to the north-west, in the country of the conquered Catuvellauni, was St. Albans—Verulamium. This had earthworks dating from before the invasion. But the other two towns were entirely unfortified, in Colchester all the effort being directed towards amenities, and in Londinium to trade.

The triangle formed by these three towns was the heart of the new province. It was screened from the rest of Britain by client kingdoms. The establishment of such vassal states was a stage in colonisation which had been proved successful in other parts of the Empire. The principle was as follows: The rulers were left in power. It was in their interest to see that their people behaved themselves, their own positions depending upon this. For further encouragement they might be assisted by financial loans or grants. This form of control suited the Romans, who were bound to be over-extended in a new country, and did not want to have too much on their hands at once. It relieved them, for instance, from the cares of local government. It was only a temporary arrangement. The states could be completely taken over and digested into the province one by one on suitable occasions in the future, such as at the death of the reigning monarch. They were not told this, of course.

The states of the eleven kings who submitted to Claudius were among those which formed a buffer for the prosperous south-east. Icenia was one. Safe at last from the ambitions of neighbouring tribes, Prasutagus could be counted upon to follow the Roman line. Brigantia was another, or at least that part of it over which Queen Cartimanḍua had authority. Her violently anti-Roman husband was a cause for anxiety, but the Queen, who had proved her loyalty by handing over Caractacus, provided a certain amount of security to the north. So the buffer of passivity swung down through the lands of Dobuni and Atrebates to Sussex by the sea where the Regni observed the obligations which King Cogidubnus had accepted. And Kent was firmly under the Roman heel. All in all, the south-east was well protected by the British themselves. But the Welsh, of course, were outside the pale.

Suetonius Paulinus would have learned this much before he left Rome. He would also have been informed of the disposition of the army, while the details of its deployment, and above all the efficiency of the legions and auxiliaries, was his over-riding interest when he reached Britain. Exactly where the units were then located we do not know. Lincoln was the headquarters of the IX Legion, Leicester of the VIII. The II Legion may have been near Gloucester. The XIV was, or had been in the time of Scapula, near Shrewsbury. The XX was somewhere in the frontier area. There were,

18. A bronze statue, found in Suffolk, is thought to represent the young Nero, who was the Roman Emperor at the time of Boadicea's revolt.

19-20. Julius Caesar, whose head appears on the coin to the right, was the first of the Romans to invade Britain, in 55-54 B.C. Nero's coins (left) would have been used in Britain at the time of Boadicea's revolt. The toy figures were found at Colchester, capital of Roman Britain, in the grave of a child who was buried about ten years before the revolt.

21. A map of Roman Britain shows the British tribes and the Roman towns and roads before and after Boadicea's revolt.

ROMAN BRITAIN

■ Principal towns
⋯ Principal roads
▲ Roman forts

Scale: 1 inch to 75 miles

VALLUM ANTONINI

OTADINI

SELGOVAE

NOVANTAE

VALLUM HADRIANI

BRIGANTES
Isurium Brigantum
Eburacum

APPROXIMATE LIMIT OF THE ROMAN ADVANCE IN 60 A.D.

Lindum

Deva

DEGEANGLI

CORNOVII
Viroconium Cornoviorum

Ratae Coritanorum

CORITANI

ICENI
Venta Icenorum

ORDOVICES

TRINOVANTES

DEMETAE

SILURES

Isca

Glevum

DOBUNI
Corinium Dobunorum

CATUVELLAUNI

Verulamium

Camulodunum

Calleva Atrebatum

Londinium

Durovernum Cantiacorum

ATREBATES

CANTIACI

Aquae Sulis

BELGAE

Venta Belgarum

REGNI

DUMNONII
Isca Dumnoniorum

DUROTRIGES

Durnovaria

Noviomagus

22. Tombstone of Longinus, found at Colchester. He was an officer of the First Squadron of Thracian cavalry, and had served fifteen years in the Roman armies before his death. It is thought that in destroying Colchester Boadicea's troops knocked off the head while leaving the cowering figure of a defeated Britain under the horse.

besides, cavalry units and auxiliaries making up a total of about 50,000 armed men.

The five legions which Suetonius had under his command, and most of the auxiliary troops besides, were all facing outward from the secure south-east. They could be switched at a marching rate of twenty miles a day, or even faster in an emergency, for a good road system had already been constructed.

The Fosse Way stretched from Exeter to Lincoln. Thus the Fosse Way was the long side of the (roughly) right-angled triangle which formed the province, the other two sides being the east and south coasts. From London a number of roads radiated to points on the Fosse Way, and in some cases beyond it. Only three are of importance here, and all were improvements or extensions of existing ancient tracks. One was Ermine Street, which ran north to Lincoln and beyond. The north-western artery was Watling Street, which crossed the Fosse Way at High Cross (Venonae) and led towards Chester, though it had not yet reached that town at the time of Suetonius's arrival. The south-western highway from London led through Silchester and Ilchester to Exeter, the southern extremity of the Fosse Way.

The past tense has been used, but the present would be applicable, for this is part of the skeleton of our present road system. Watling Street, with which we will be mainly concerned, is the A5, which leads to Holyhead. The later Roman road did the same, but at the time when Suetonius became Governor it stopped short of Wales.

One more road of the period must be mentioned. Chester was connected with Gloucester. This route ran roughly parallel with the eastern extremity of the Welsh mountains.

Suetonius was fortunate to inherit a province which had adequate communications. Such roads took time to build. In nothing does Roman thoroughness stand out more clearly than in their road-making. The causeway, about sixteen feet across and drained by lateral ditches when necessary, was dug down to a firm foundation. On this was laid a nine inch thickness of flat stones, then an equal thickness of brick and stone bound with lime concrete. The roads were aligned by instrument and by smoke signals, and if they had to change direction it was done on the crest of a rise. The labour both for construction and mainte-nance was provided by the local communities, only the surveyors, engineers and supervisors being Romans. These solidly built avenues, fit for any traffic in any weather, cut straight and purposefully through the thickly-forested countryside and over the downland.

The result of this road system was that news from Gloucester could be carried to the central London-St. Albans-Colchester area in two or three days by relays of messengers riding day and night. A legion could cover the distance in a week, its heavy baggage following by wagon. And even Chester was less than twice as far away in time. This may at first reaction appear slow to our motor-conditioned minds. But East and West had never been so close before. The legions marched with full equipment. Their uniform was armoured, and they wore it whether fighting or not—when digging their protective camps, for instance. The legionary had a metal helmet and a cuirass of thick leather furnished with metal strips. His main protection was his shield, a long semi-cylinder of heavy leather with a central boss projecting in front. Held close to the body it covered him from chin to knees, while the boss could be used as a punch against close opposition. His weapons were a short sword, a dagger and two seven-foot

javelins. He carried, besides, two sharpened
stakes and an entrenching tool which were used
for the construction of the ditch and palisade
which encircled the marching camps. And he
carried a mess tin and a fortnight's ration of
corn. For the Roman legionary was a vegetarian
and only ate meat, grumblingly, when there
was nothing else. His total load was about
sixty pounds. That he was able to march
twenty miles a day and then fortify a camp
before he cooked, ate and slept is a measure of
the fitness demanded. Any failure for a reason
other than sickness or wounds was severely
dealt with.

This is a convenient place to say something
about the method of fighting. The legions
were the heart and spearpoint of the battle line.
For command, each legion of five or six
thousand men was divided into cohorts of
about five hundred. Each cohort comprised
six centuries—actually of eighty men. The
legions advanced, or awaited the enemy, in
open order so that the throwing arm was free.
When the two forces were within forty yards of
each other the first javelin was cast. The
second was delivered as soon as possible after
that. If the enemy was charging, the range
would by then be twenty yards or less. A

well-thrown javelin either transfixed an enemy or pierced his shield. In the latter case the effect was almost as deadly as the first. The point was of hard metal, but the shank was of soft iron and bent under the weight of the long wooden shaft. It was as a result impossible in the time available to pull it out of the shield, which therefore had to be discarded.

As soon as the second javelin had been thrown the order was given to close ranks. The legionaries came together almost shield to shield. They lowered their helmeted heads and shuffled forward in a jog-trot charge. The bosses of the shields butted into the enemy ranks. Between the shields the short sharp swords flicked and stabbed. An unarmoured enemy was then at a terrible disadvantage, whereas the legionaries were covered in every vital part.

By trumpet call the formation or direction of attack could be changed. The legions were meticulously drilled. The wedge formation was commonly used. One may imagine how it could split up a barbaric horde. The British tribesmen's swords were long and made for slashing only. The points were not sharpened. They were of little use against these close-packed armoured wedges. Nor had the tribes the organization, training or discipline to change their form of attack or defence in the middle of a battle. There was no single combat here, nothing to which they were accustomed— half-naked man against half-naked man. They were opposed by a multi-pronged killing machine directed by trumpet blast.

As soon as the enemy wavered, or if they held firm in places, the wings of Roman cavalry, the *alae*, were brought in, charging with lances. And the auxiliaries, men of conquered continental tribes, let loose their sling bolts and arrows.

It is not surprising that the Romans never lost a pitched battle in Britain. But although they were left in possession of the field they by no means always followed up successfully. Only the cavalry could catch a lightly-accoutred fleeing enemy, and the cavalry were comparatively few in numbers.

In skirmishes the legionaries often had the worst of it. If they could be caught off guard in an ambush or by a rush from cover, before they had time to form up, a swift enemy could do serious damage and get away again. This was the sort of fighting that Caractacus had led after being beaten in the pitched battle of the Medway. These raids continued. And when

the Romans penetrated into the Welsh mountains they were up against other difficulties as
well. They did not know the country, and
their heavy baggage trains could not follow
the mountain trails. Besides, they were at a
disadvantage to these tough little Celts in their
own climate.

Wonderful as was the strength and fitness
of the legionaries they lacked the sheer stamina
and ferocious determination of the Welshman.
It was said the Celts could live on roots, could
crouch all day up to their necks in water and
take no harm from it. Probably the stories
were exaggerated, but they show the respect
that the well-armed Romans had developed for
their mountain enemies.

There were three Welsh tribes which the
Romans at that period encountered. The
Silures were in the south-east, above the
Bristol Channel and the Severn estuary. The
Ordovices, a large tribe, covered the mountain-
ous area between Snowdonia and Wroxeter on
the upper Severn. The Degeangli lived in
Flintshire.

It was as war leader of the Silures that
Caractacus had made such damaging raids
through the Roman lines before he moved
north-westward into the country of the

Ordovices for his final and disastrous battle.
Both tribes had ever since been implacably
hostile to the invaders. The Ordovici, living
further removed among their mountains, had
had less direct contact with the Romans. But
the Silures had never ceased from bothering,
and although each military governor after
Plautius had tried to impress them with the
might of Rome, the Silures had managed to
cause quite as much damage as they suffered.

That was the background on which Suetonius
could make his military appreciation. Like
Veronius, he had a free hand regarding further
conquest—so long as he made the province
pay. This was all the more urgent after so much
time had been wasted. The problem of the
Celts in Wales took priority over any other that
might exist in the rest of the country.

Suetonius was not a young man when he
came to Britain. He was a hardened veteran.
We have authoritative information on his
governorship, since Agricola, the father-in-law
of Tacitus, was on his staff. We are not told
very many details, but enough to piece together
the General's plan. Briefly this was to converge
upon the heart of Welsh resistance. The final
fortress was Snowdonia in the far north-west.
And behind Snowdonia lay Anglesey, a fertile

island which provided food and respite for the warriors.

The similarity with the conditions which had existed in Mauritania was striking—fields of corn out of harm's way behind the range. But Anglesey was more than that. It had become the refuge of all who would not endure the Roman yoke, and it was the stronghold of the Druids.

How to get at it? The old soldier did not underestimate the difficulties. Snowdonia was not as high as the Atlas range, but it was rugged, its climate was much worse, and tracks were rudimentary. The Roman lines of communication would be very long and difficult to defend in the mountain section. Anglesey, the goal and the only place where food could be obtained if hostilities were prolonged, was separated from the mainland by a sea channel. The presence of the sea introduced a factor which had not been present in the Mauritanian campaign. On the one hand it complicated the final assault; on the other it provided a further opportunity for outflanking the mountains. Rome had a small fleet in southern British waters. Suetonius ordered it up via Bristol and the Outer Ocean and made a base at Chester which was then—before the River Dee silted up—an excellent natural harbour.

It is important to make plain how extended was the Roman line of communications and how deeply committed were the fighting forces. Suetonius had with him two legions, the XIV and the XX. With a large number of auxiliaries and additional forces his army may have numbered 25,000 men—half of Rome's total strength in Britain. The other half had to police the indefinite northern frontier, South Wales, the still uncertain tribes south of the Bristol Channel, and the whole of the south-east. Nor was this only for a short period. It took Suetonius two campaigning seasons to complete his pincer movement round Snowdonia and mass his forces for the final assault across the Menai Straits.

Part of his army, starting from Chester, followed the north coast of Wales through Flintshire. By what route the other part advanced south of Snowdonia we do not know. The walker and the motorist may make their guesses how his troops and baggage train found a way from Wroxeter or elsewhere on the upper Severn to Portmadoc on the west coast. But in the spring of 60 A.D. all that remained of Suetonius's army in Wales was drawn up on the shore facing Anglesey. They had with them flat-bottomed boats built in the new yards at Chester and towed into position by the fleet. Facing them across the strip of water was the hard core of British resistance, military and religious. It was literally a last ditch stand—except that the Menai Straits are more considerable than any ditch.

The infantry were carried across on the flat-bottomed boats. The cavalry swam with their horses.... From water level, as every swimmer knows, the shore seems further than it is, and in any case 300 yards is a long swim. The young Agricola vividly remembered the scene, and the impression it made upon him is conveyed in the written description of Tacitus.

The shores of Anglesey swarmed with armed men. The Roman soldiers were used to barbarian hordes. But this was different. Among the warriors were Druid priests who raised their arms to heaven, shouting prayers and curses. There were fanatical women dressed in black, their hair dishevelled and with torches in their hands, who ran about screaming and shouting in an ecstacy of fury.

The Romans were superstitious. For all their conviction of superiority they never went into battle until the auguries had been considered. Presumably the signs had been favourable. But, up to their necks in water or borne on this strange element in little boats, they were faced by something utterly unknown and terrifying. "This weird spectacle," wrote Tacitus, "awed the Roman soldiers into a kind of paralysis."

If the Britons had then possessed a leader of the quality of Caractacus he would undoubtedly have led an attack, in the water or on it in coracles. But there was no attack, and the Roman trumpets blared. That harsh material noise had given the orders in battle drill since every veteran was a recruit. The legionaries vaulted overboard and splashed ashore, javelins poised. The cavalry mounted their staggering horses and formed up. They charged.

There was little effective resistance. Fanat-icism is no counter once the fear of it is overcome. The multitude of men and women, soldiers and priests, was stabbed down and trampled under foot. The Roman army swept on to loot and pillage and burn and massacre and cut down the sacred groves of the Druids.

One cannot avoid trying to imagine the feelings of Suetonius at this moment. It is given to few to be the victor of two exceptionally difficult campaigns. As a young man he had conquered Mauritania. Now, well past middle age, he had reduced the furthest corner of Britain.

Whatever were his feelings, they quickly changed. An exhausted messenger delivered a rolled parchment. Rebellion had broken out in Icenia, two hundred miles behind him.

V

FIRE IN THE EAST

Much had happened in East Anglia while Suetonius had been in the west. Seeds of trouble planted long before had sprouted and grown harvest ripe, while other damaging weeds had sprung up more quickly.

One such sowing had been the disarming of the tribes by Ostorius Scapula ten years before. Although the resistance to this by the Iceni had quickly been suppressed, it cannot be supposed they had forgotten. Besides, they and their neighbours would be most unlikely to hand over all their weapons—any more than the Scottish Highlanders did after the Jacobite rising of 1745—and in any case ample replacements could have been made and concealed during the following decade.

The indifference of the Romans to this danger, and to that caused by other provocations which will be mentioned, was due to their conviction of superiority. They were the best organizers in the world, with the best army. They were a civilization, and scorned the barbarians. They took scant notice of human feelings. Icenia, for instance, was due to be absorbed into the province on the death of its king. Then Roman-type towns would be built with temple, senate house, theatre—as was done at Colchester. The youth of good families would be educated in Roman schools, trained in the Roman army. Latin would become the official language, gradually replacing the indigenous tongue. Slowly perhaps, but surely the Iceni would be Romanized.

If they were foolish enough to revolt at any time they would quickly be crushed. A legion was stationed at Lincoln, not far from their borders, and there were small garrisons in forts at strategic points. Rome had no fear of a single tribe and believed the British incapable of uniting. Had they not been squabbling like cats and dogs before the invasion? And had they not proved that they were helpless since then? The Romanization could proceed unhurriedly, as planned, and meanwhile the tribes would pay for the amenities of civilization which were being brought to them.

These payments were another source of trouble. For both the people of the province and the client kingdoms they were by no means light. Their labour or their lives as soldiers

91

might be required of them. They were taxed
on their lands, their property, their trade, and
were forced to provide corn at fixed rates to
feed their conquerors. It seems likely also that
during the brief governorship of Veranius, or
at the start of his successor's, a census was made
and a revision of taxes ordered. Not only were
the official taxes high, but the Roman bureau-
crats did not scruple to squeeze out something
extra for themselves. There were also Roman
businessmen, private money-lenders, prepared
to make loans, at high interest, to those who
found difficulty in paying what was demanded
of them. Dio tells us that Seneca, Nero's
counsellor and former tutor, had forty million
sesterces—about £40,000—out on private loan
in Britain. This may not be true, but certainly
the new province was being increasingly
exploited in a variety of ways, and the client
kingdoms scarcely less.

But if the eyes of the Procurator and the
Roman businessmen were on Icenia, this was
because they considered it worth exploiting.
In the 50's the tribe must have been as prosperous
as at any time in its history. Prasutagus is
spoken of by Tacitus as rich, and there is no
reason to doubt it. Ever since the revolt of
48 there had been peace with Rome and security

from the once-threatening Belgae. The agricultural revolution brought about by the iron-shod plough had borne fruit. The Icenian landowners were growing more corn than ever before. But their greatest riches were probably their flocks and herds, and their hardy little horses.

The large landowners were the aristocracy, many of whom were connected with the royal house. Boadicea is quoted by Dio as speaking with scorn about the softness and luxury of the Roman way of life. But the Icenian nobles did themselves well enough. We have no way of knowing where the royal palace was. Caister near Norwich is of later date, though there might have been an earlier settlement there. Professor Dudley has suggested the Thetford area, though archaeology has so far failed to settle this question. This negative evidence suggests that the Icenian capital was neither large nor built of durable materials.

Of more interest is the Icenian royal family. All that we know from the records about Prasutagus has already been mentioned—that he had a long and prosperous reign. Being of great possessions he would be inclined to be cautious: the *status quo* suited him best. Such would be the ideal monarch from the point of view of the Governor. Prasutagus could be relied on to keep his people in order, leaving Suetonius free for his adventures in the west. The point of view of the Procurator might well be different—but of him later.

It is a little difficult to picture Boadicea as the wife of Prasutagus. She is a vivid personality after all these centuries, he no more than a vague shadow of a type. A woman with the qualities of generalship, with the passion and the courage of the rebel, would not naturally ally herself, one would have thought, with the sort of person we have pictured as the king. "She was huge of frame," says Dio, "terrifying of aspect, and with a harsh voice." He was describing her later on, when there was reason for her aspect to have changed and her voice hardened. But the big frame was there already. However, if Prasutagus married a large and dominating woman he would not be the only mild man to have done so. And it may well be that the qualities which Boadicea was later to reveal were at that time hidden, for there had not yet been cause to bring them out. At the time we are dealing with she must have been in her thirties. So she would only have been a teen-aged girl during the tribal squabbles before the invasion.

She and Prasutagus had two daughters. We do not know their names, and we can only guess at their ages. Judging by the probable date of their parents' marriage, the elder was perhaps fifteen or sixteen in 59—not more; the younger a year or two less. We know from our own experience of monarchy that the family life of the royal house is of great sentimental interest to the people. The Iceni were to demonstrate a very lively sympathy for their Queen and princesses, so it is not extravagant to suppose that it was a happy family. Although we are deducing on scant evidence, Boadicea can be imagined in character as well as appearance. The features and garments which Dio describes—bright red hair which fell to her knees, a big gold chain, a brooch to hold her outer mantle and a dress of many colours— would fit a robust person who enjoyed life as well as a fiery warrior. One cannot know which character fitted her more naturally, but one must admit that either is possible.

The lightly-built chariot with its two lively horses was the state coach of the day, as much as it was an instrument of war. There was scarcely room for more than two in a chariot; so one may suppose that when the Queen and the princesses rode abroad, one of them must have been the driver. Driving fast, without roads, without springs, was a fiercely athletic, even acrobatic skill. If the Queen drove in a tribe of charioteers she must have driven well. One can picture this big, strong woman standing balanced on the bumping car, leaning forward with the reins in both hands, shouting to her horses, her face alight, her hair flying.... As for the colour of her hair, all which was not black or blond was, to dark-complexioned conquerors, red. (Much later, the Chinese called the British "the red-headed Barbarians.") So the bright hair was possibly no more brilliant than chestnut. But of whatever colour, hair a yard long and streaming in the wind—it is a picture! And the two young girls, freckled perhaps and happy, clinging tightly and laughing as the chariot swerved and jumped—one does not need to be sentimental to see with the mind's eye a picture of barbaric domesticity which catches the imagination.

The census would cause a loss of privacy, an invasion of inquisitive agents, for the main purpose was to make an all-round evaluation. Tacitus is surely referring to increases of taxes and perhaps conscription too when he summarises the complaints of the British in these words: "That the only effect of their patience was more grievous impositions upon a people who submitted with such facility. Formerly they had one king over them; now there were two, the Governor and the Procurator, the former venting his rage upon their life's blood, the latter on their property. The union or discord of these two was equally fatal to those whom they ruled, while the officers of the one and the centurions [the old soldiers of the *colonia*] of the other joined in oppressing them by all kinds of violence and contumely, so that nothing was safe from their avarice, nothing from their lust."

Extortion rather than legal tax collection is strongly suggested. It is also pertinent that the union or discord of the Governor and Procurator are referred to. There is ample evidence that Suetonius and Catus did not like each other. Suetonius was a ruthless general, capable of great cruelty, but one does not fail to detect nobleness in his behaviour. In Catus there was none. In every reference to him he comes out as gracelessly cruel and avaricious. The Governor, while in East Anglia, would have imposed a certain restraint and caution on the Procurator, but he was in Wales.

It must have been common gossip among the

men of business who were Roman citizens or cognizant of imperial custom that Icenia would be absorbed on the death of her king. Rome had always shown that she was entirely cynical about the peoples whom she ruled or meant to rule. They were, so to speak, fattened up in a state of semi-freedom, and then when the time was ripe, engulfed and digested. The death of the monarch was a generally suitable occasion. Therefore if Prasutagus became ill, or if there were any doubt about his health, those who had private funds invested in that kingdom would want to retrieve them before they were absorbed by Rome. Certain it is that there was a descent of usurers on Icenia intent on getting their money back.

Troubles rarely come singly. The Procurator saw what was happening, and was in a position to know the imperial intention. Whether or not he had funds of his own to call in, he was responsible for seeing that Rome got her full share. At the time of the submission of the eleven kings, the Emperor Claudius had made certain grants—economic aid to buy co-operation. Catus decided to treat these as loans and to call them in, plus the unpaid interest of more than fifteen years. This alone would have been crippling, but it was not the only exaction. Tacitus quotes the Iceni as complaining that their houses were seized and their children forced away from them, presumably as conscripts or slaves. As for the Trinovantes, they had trouble enough. The veterans of the *colonia* "were ejecting the inhabitants from their houses, and driving them from their lands, calling them slaves and captives; in which high-handed proceedings they were encouraged by the soldiers, whose lives were like their own, and who looked forward to a similar licence for themselves."

The soldiers referred to were those still with the colours who had been detailed as guard for the Procurator. There were not many of them. The Governor had taken to the west every man he could. But it appears that those whom Catus had under his command were of a similar type to himself, more interested in spoils than war.

When things turn from good to bad, and from bad to worse the sufferer may reach a stage at which he feels that there is nothing more unpleasant left to happen. But what the Iceni had endured was only a prelude to what lay in store for them. The unhappy year 59 was not yet over when Prasutagus died.

Cautious to the end, he had left a will by

which half of his great fortune went to the Emperor Nero. The half remaining was to be divided between his daughters. His widow inherited nothing. We have some record in Tacitus and Dio of Boadicea's sayings in the months which followed. There is no evidence whatever that she was in any way aggrieved. It is at least possible that she knew the terms of her husband's will while he was still alive, and that she approved of his intention. This, clearly, was voluntarily to pay so great a death duty that imperial Rome would be satisfied and leave the Iceni in peace. Tacitus says as much: Prasutagus acted in this way "in the belief that this mark of attention would result in the kingdom and his household being left alone."

Nothing happened immediately. Both the Procurator and the men of business had their agents already in the country. The extortions in the name of rightful recovery continued, with sequestration of property from those who could not pay. News of the king's death, and the terms of his will, had to be carried to Rome, and an answer received. Thus there was no change during the winter months, which in any case were unsuitable for travel. The Governor would have been informed within a week or two of what had happened, even if he was in Chester or the furthest corner of Wales. Settlement of the Icenian question was a matter of government. It was much more than fiscal, and therefore out of the province of the Procurator. Furthermore Suetonius must have known that Catus was a crook. But his eyes were set on Anglesey and the completion of his campaign. He never looked over his shoulder.

Catus went into Icenia with the strongest force he could collect. This consisted of some regular troops and a number of the old soldiers—Tacitus calls them centurions—from the *colonia* at Colchester. In Icenia they joined forces with those already in that kingdom. So far Catus was technically within his rights: he was on his way to collect the legacy due to Nero. But his interpretation of Prasutagus's will put his action beyond all reason. He considered that not only half of the dead king's estate belonged to the Emperor, but all of it; and he ruled that the estate was not only the personal possessions of the deceased but the whole kingdom. He took the lands and property of the nobles and carried off the able bodied as slaves.

The climax was the behaviour of his men

at the royal palace. Tacitus does not mention fighting, but even if Boadicea was in some way deprived of her guard she would not take such an intrusion quietly. We already know something of these centurions. "Nothing was exempted from their avarice, nothing from their lust." Resistance by someone they considered of an inferior race, and particularly by a woman, would only incite them further. What Boadicea did one would dearly like to know. One feels sure that she at least slapped their faces. This big woman must have been very angry. But she was overpowered and bound. She was flogged. And her young daughters were raped. Then these not-so-noble Romans departed with all the loot they could carry.

It was remarked briefly in the Preface that the rebellion of Boadicea was marked by atrocious cruelties. This is the moment to weigh that up. If a mother of today saw her daughters raped by hooligans, would her feelings be less violent than those of a mother of two thousand years ago? Would she not want to kill? If she could not do that, she would have the law to aid her. For Boadicea there was no man-made law, but she had the power of her tribe behind her passion. Their homes had also been looted and one supposes there had been sexual outrage in other households. The wild men of Catus were out on the spree. Their behaviour with the Queen and her daughters would be for the Celts like a torch thrown into dry straw.

The wonder is that there was not an immediate outburst. Had that resulted it would no doubt have been quickly suppressed. The mother's fury would have flared and died, leaving no trace in history. But Boadicea possessed qualities which even she may have been unaware of at the time. As a first step she controlled herself, and found that she could also control her naturally undisciplined supporters. Then her power must have dawned on her, and she set to work with the skill of an experienced general.

One would give a great deal for an Icenian description of the months that followed. We have only the Roman historian, Tacitus, laconic and biased; and Dio, sometimes verbose but quite as biased. But the achievements of this remarkable woman are set down and we have only to assess them.

Spring had come. Tacitus says, later, that the Britons did not sow corn that season because they expected to have taken over the

Roman supplies by autumn. This does not ring true. Farmers would always sow their fields if they could. Besides, the Roman supplies were of British corn. Probably the sowing was hindered or prevented by the troops and pillage gangs of Catus.

It is true, however, that the Icenians were busy with other matters besides farming. "Relieved from present dread by the absence of the Governor," says Tacitus, "the Britons began to hold conferences in which they painted the miseries of servitude, compared their several injuries, and inflamed each other..." The participants are spoken of as Britons, not exclusively Icenians. The representatives of other tribes must have been involved from an early stage. But these conferences were held on Icenian soil. Their country was surrounded by the sea, by the Fen marshland and by forest except for the narrow chalk strip; and this strip had been left barren in the Newmarket area as protection against the once hostile Trinovantes. These obstacles had been the natural defences of the Iceni against attack by their neighbours. Now they made the country an ideal rallying ground for counter-attack against the common invader. One must imagine agents and representatives slipping through the forest or crossing the Fens by tracks known only to local guides. Later, when the representatives had been won over, forces of fighting strength would begin to converge by the same routes.

All this was organized with extraordinary skill. The Romans had a well-developed intelligence service which included a widespread network of spies. But they discovered nothing about the preliminary moves.

Before saying more about these preparations we must decide who was in charge and by what right. Boadicea was the inspiration, and it was she who led the army when it formed. But it is open to question whether she had, by virtue of her position, the right to lead even the Icenian section. She was the widow of the king, the queen mother. It is just possible that she was the queen regnant and that Prasutagus had become king by marrying her, or as a nominee of the Romans; but there is nothing to support this. No coinage has been found bearing Boadicea's name or image, or that of her husband. There is no numismatic clue. Nor have we a precedent for Icenian royal inheritance. In neighbouring tribes the kingdom went to the eldest son, or was divided between the sons. But Boadicea was certainly treated as their ruling queen by the Iceni. And she was accepted as war-leader by all the tribes. She was elected to this position as Caractacus had been in Wales and Vercingetorix in Gaul. Since she had no previous experience in war this must have been from force of her personality and ability in conference.

The Celtic tribes were notoriously individualistic, yet she welded a confederacy. Meanwhile there were weapons, stores and men to be collected and a plan of campaign to be worked out—all in complete secrecy. The first objective was Colchester. Camulodunum was the capital of Roman Britain, the centre of its culture. The temple of Claudius was symbolic of imperial rule, god-like in its omnipotence. Most compelling of all, in Colchester were the centurions who had done the outrage.

While the army was mustering, a form of psychological warfare was launched against Colchester. "At this time," wrote Tacitus, "for no understandable reason the statue of Victory at Camulodunum fell down, with its back turned as if flying from the enemy. Frenzied women sang of coming destruction. Weird cries were heard in the senate house and inhuman howlings in the theatre. An image of the colony in ruins was seen in the estuary. A blood-red ocean and the impressions of human bodies left by the receding tide were interpreted as hopeful signs for the Britons and omens of disaster for the veterans."

However these things were contrived, they had a powerful effect. The roughest men are often the most superstitious. They began worrying about the town's lack of defences. But when they made plans for the building of moat and rampart they were persuaded that these were unnecessary. The local Britons were if possible more passive and subservient than ever. It was impossible to imagine trouble in the heart of the province after seventeen years of peace.

The Celt is quickly roused to passion, and no doubt was all the more inflammable then. How he was made to hide his feelings so that the Roman intelligence was deceived is a mystery. Meanwhile, Boadicea was swelling her forces by fiery speeches and cogent arguments. We do not know all the tribes which joined the Iceni. The Trinovantes certainly did, some of the Catuvellauni of the St. Albans district probably, and perhaps detachments from the Durotriges of Dorset, from the Dobuni to the north of them, from the Coritani, and from the Brigantes and the Parisii from as far afield as Yorkshire. Certainly the Governor was in Wales with half the army. But there remained a legion in Gloucester, another on the upper Severn, another in Lincoln. Also there were occupied forts on all the roads, and detachments in Colchester, London, St. Albans. There were spies everywhere. Yet Boadicea managed without detection to concentrate an army which Dio says numbered 120,000 men.

This is probably an exaggeration, but the host must have been enormous, for the Celt went to war with his wife, children and domestic animals. War was a family affair. Certainly the country was thickly forested, but it almost passes belief that such an undisciplined multitude could have been gathered together, and kept secret, under the Roman noses of the authorities. Yet it is a Roman historian who states it.

One cannot say that Boadicea had chosen her time well, for events had forced her to action. But the timing was favourable to her. Suetonius was poised for his final attack in Wales, all his resources, all his supporting troops looking towards Anglesey. And because this was his objective—Mona, the sacred island of the

Druids—the cult of Druidism supported the Queen. Although officially suppressed, there were Druid priests throughout the land. Their influence and oratory must have helped considerably in the enlistment.

It was probably April or May when Suetonius was in position to attack Anglesey and Boadicea felt ready to lead her army southwards. It is at this stage that Dio gives the description of her which has already been quoted in part. She stood on a rostrum in the middle of the host, her face terrifying in its fury, her voice harsh, her bright hair hanging to her knees. "She wore a great twisted golden necklace, and a tunic of many colours, over which was a thick mantle fastened by a brooch. Now she grasped a spear to strike fear into all who watched her…"

The speech which Dio puts into her mouth is very long and not very impressive—a recapitulation of all the grievances, all the hopes. It is almost certainly invented by the historian and therefore best left unquoted. But imagination needs no stimulus to picture the scene as this big woman with long hair and blazing eyes made the final call to battle.

VI

THE FIRE GETS OUT
OF CONTROL

When Boadicea's followers poured down from the forests of Norfolk and Suffolk into Essex the well-kept secret of the rebellion was out. Its strength and direction of thrust were known. The host swept past military posts, ignoring them as an incoming tide flows around rocks later to be submerged. From these strong points, when left alone again, must have gone the gallopers who brought the news to Suetonius in Wales and Cerialis at Lincoln.

Suetonius Paulinus is a particularly interesting character in contrast to Boadicea. We know more about him than we do of the queen, for Agricola's admiration for his general flows through the stylus of his son-in-law. Tacitus in any case had great respect for the characteristics of ancient Rome, many of which were possessed by Suetonius. He was on the one hand a careful and thorough organizer, exacting in discipline and the precision of battle drill. On the other he was a man who took risks. He was personally fearless to the point of foolhardiness. He had the reputation of always taking a personal part in the battles where he commanded. And he could stake his reputation and the thousands of lives for which he was responsible as unemotionally as a gambler putting chips on a number. Human lives meant nothing in themselves. If he was not actively cruel, he was without sympathy for suffering. He was hard, efficient. Also he was ambitious, a rival of Corbulo who had won a great name in Armenia. He was a soldier first and last, a governor only by appointment. Law and civil administration were of far less interest to him than military concerns. Finally, Suetonius was not a young man. To do what he did in late middle age he must have been exceptionally hard in body as well as mind. Britain would be his last command. His reputation would stand or fall by what he achieved.

He had done what his predecessors had failed to do, captured the granary of Wales and the stronghold of the Druids. But the news which he then received nullified this victory. It looked as if he had won the Island of Anglesey at the cost of the Island of Britain. That would happen unless he moved very

quickly and Boadicea slowly. She was within
a few miles of Colchester, within easy reach of
London and St. Albans. He was two hundred
and seventy miles away. She was reported to
have over 100,000 followers, fresh men at the
start of a campaign. The army he had led into
Wales had been reduced by casualties and was
tired. In any case all this force could not be
turned against the queen, for although the
enemy in Anglesey had been wiped out there
were still plenty of Welshmen in the mountains.
The same restriction applied to possible
reinforcements from the legionary bases at
Gloucester, Wroxeter, Lincoln. Even if these
forces could be concentrated, few men could
be spared from police duties in these areas.
The spirit of revolt might spread like an
epidemic, particularly if the garrisons were
moved.

Suetonius weighed the chances and took his
decision. It was too late to help Colchester, but
London might be saved if he could get there
before Boadicea. Speed was more important
than numbers. He had with him in Wales the
XIV and XX Legions. The infantry could not
reach London in much less than a fortnight,
by which time the British host would almost
certainly be there. So he rode off with the

cavalry, ordering the infantry to follow him.

This was bold, quite apart from the fact that he would have to ride through potentially hostile country all the way. His striking force was small. Each legion had on its establishment little more than a hundred horsemen. He had with him, too, some of the auxiliary cavalry, units of 500 enlisted from conquered territories on the continent. But the total is unlikely to have exceeded fifteen hundred. In any case cavalry alone would be of limited value, particularly for defending a town. That he might as soon as possible achieve a more balanced force he sent gallopers to the II Legion at Gloucester ordering it to meet him on the road. As for food stores and baggage, they would travel even more slowly than the infantry, at the pace of mules or oxen. For two or three weeks each soldier would have to depend upon what he carried.

We do not know what route Suetonius followed. But the most direct available to him was Watling Street. If he took it, one may suppose that he ordered II Legion to meet him at High Cross, where the Fosse Way coming up from Gloucestershire crosses Watling Street. There is doubt on the detail of all Suetonius's movements, as there is of Boadicea's, for neither Tacitus nor Dio give itineraries. This matters comparatively little to the general reader, and the position of the rendezvous ordered for II Legion matters least of all, for it was not kept.

When the gallopers from North Wales reached Gloucester the Legate of II Legion was not in command, being ill or absent on some operation. In his place was the Camp Prefect, Poenius Postumus. He refused to move the legion. So he has come down in history as a coward. Possibly he was, but it seems unlikely. He had risen from legionary— private soldier—to acting command. During the last seventeen years the legion had seen much hard fighting in Britain, first under Vespasian against the tribes of the south-west and then against the Silures, whom it still opposed. A soldier in the field does not climb the slippery pole of promotion from the ranks if he lacks physical courage, while to give a flat refusal to one's general requires moral fibre. Why Poenius Postumus disobeyed the order to march seventy units or so to the nearest point on Watling Street we shall never know. Perhaps no one knew even at the time, for he killed himself by falling on his sword after hearing of the battle he had avoided.

114

He may have anticipated a serious threat to his sector of the frontier. He may well in his own opinion have acted for the best. But the absence of II Legion destroyed the general's logistic plan which would have enabled him to reach London with a balanced force.

To the great credit of Suetonius he did not hesitate a moment. He rode straight on with the cavalry at a rate of about fifty miles a day. He was in the thickly-forested Midlands which might have concealed in ambush an enemy of twenty times his strength. Travelling with such urgency he could not have allowed himself to be slowed down to the pace of lateral patrols working through the thickets on either side of the road. At night it was Roman standing orders for the legionaries to build a marching camp protected by a seven foot ditch and a palisade. The cavalry, busy with their horses, were excused this chore. It is not to be supposed that they undertook it now, when there were no infantry. By day they clattered on at their best pace, and by night they slept under the rain or stars, still more vulnerable to attack. The only precaution which Suetonius took—which he could take in the circumstances—was to move fast, to arrive before Boadicea could expect him.

The cavalry were the élite of the Roman army. They wore brilliantly-coloured cloaks, their armour and accoutrements were highly polished. Our nearest modern equivalent is the Household Cavalry in a state procession. As they cantered down the long, straight road through the forests of the Midlands one can imagine the awe with which the half-naked woodsmen saw them pass.

One cannot help wondering what were the general's thoughts as he rode, saddle-sore, aching and tired. He could not usefully plan ahead without knowing more of the situation. In conditions of weariness and discomfort the mind is resentful. He must have been furious with Poenius Postumus. To one whose whole working life was attuned to the mechanical reactions of discipline the behaviour of this ranker officer must have been inexplicable and inexcusable. Roman law provided for a slow and painful death for one who, as Tacitus put it bluntly in this instance, "disobeyed the commands of his general, contrary to his military oath."

But the anger of Suetonius must have been directed far more fiercely against Boadicea. This is more than a guess. His subsequent behaviour displayed a vindictive cruelty which

116

went far beyond military and governmental needs. Even the materialistic Roman Senate saw this. Suetonius hated Boadicea, and through her all the Iceni. One does not know if he and she had met. It is quite possible that he saw her with Prasutagus at some governmental gathering in Colchester soon after his arrival in Britain, before he set out for the west. If so he no doubt remembered her appearance, a big, striking woman. The Romans were not large. She was very likely taller than he. And she was a barbarian, queen of a tribe he despised. He would not be favourably impressed. Now she had turned the brilliant success of his Welsh campaign upside down, made a fool of him in the eyes of Rome and the barbaric world. He must have boiled with personal indignation against her.

He reached London before her, covering five times the distance which had separated her from it at Colchester. But he did not know that in the meantime she had doubled back to fight another and harder battle.

It requires an effort of the imagination to picture London as it then was. It was scarcely older than the Roman conquest, but in recent years it had grown like a mushroom patch, too fast for the usual Roman town planning. This sheltered natural harbour within easy reach of the continent had attracted merchants from Rome, north and south Italy, Gaul, Spain, Greece, all parts of the Empire. Many had built themselves houses and settled down. The place had sprung up anyhow, a cluster of wooden houses with some superior villas. The river was full of shipping, the banks lined by wharves and sheds. The untidy little town was prosperous and busy. The imports were stores for the army and luxuries for the rich, its exports metals, hides, mastiffs, and slaves. No doubt many Britons were among the twenty or twenty-five thousand inhabitants. They had accepted the new way of life. Londinium was an international market, polyglot in speech, but to the rebellious Celts an example of Rome's handiwork and therefore to be destroyed.

When Suetonius arrived with his tired cavalry he found the *municipium* a very anxious place. The threat of death hung over the inhabitants. The Procurator, Catus, who had sparked off the rebellion, had left the Londoners to their fate and fled to Gaul. It would not have been possible for many civilians to escape to the continent on the little merchant ships, while to scatter into the country would have been as dangerous as remaining. They were branded as Roman sympathizers, and who could tell how widely the rebellion had spread? They greeted Suetonius as their saviour. He, on his side, was brought up to date with the situation—and took a different view.

It is convenient to describe what had happened during the last fortnight or so from the point of view of Boadicea.

She marched straight on Colchester. For her it stood for the men who had outraged her family, for all the Iceni the same. For the Trinovantes it stood for their slave masters. For the other tribal contingents its Temple of Claudius was the symbol of Roman conquest. But although the objective was clear and approved of by all, the host would travel slowly. If its numbers were anything approaching the 120,000 recorded, the column would stretch on a road for well over thirty miles. Apart from other considerations, this gives reason to doubt Dio's estimate. But, divided by three or four, the column remains unwieldy. As anyone who has travelled in a big convoy knows, the speed is slower than the individual speed of the slowest—whatever mathematics may say! If one imagines the

waggons carrying food and families, the picture
is an organizational nightmare. How long, for
instance, would it take to camp and break
camp, to halt for rest and food and start again?
In a military command orders pass quickly
down a chain of subordinates to every man.
With a collection of tribal units held together
only by enthusiasm there would be less of a
chain than a tangle. Boadicea had been elected
war-leader, but she would have to depend on
tact and inspiration in place of discipline.
When considered realistically, what she achieved
appears supernatural.

As she started southwards in her chariot
after the long and anxious period of secret
preparations, she must have felt the intoxication
of having swayed a multitude with her words.
Then the problems of leadership would begin.
What these were will be best conveyed by
looking more closely at the composition of the
host. Not only was it made up of tribal
detachments, but each detachment was sub-
divided under its nobles or strong men.
Rivalries would be inevitable, and the tribes
themselves had been at war within the memory
of many. Quarrels or arguments about
precedence would be inevitable. There was no
uniformity in equipment. The nobles were

well-armed and armoured—if they had managed
to save their weapons from confiscation. The
simple men had hunting spears, bows and
arrows, home-made swords, clubs. Some were
on horseback and most on foot. The waggons
had different loads and draught animals. They
carried women and children and food—food
for the multitude must have been an endless
problem. It is interesting to conjecture
whether there were women in the fighting
force. It is put forward with diffidence that some
of the refinements of killing and mutilation
recorded by the Roman historians suggest the
feminine touch. In later history, both among
the North American Indians and in the East, it
was the women whom the captives chiefly
feared. And in this case the Iceni had reason—
among other things—to hate the enemy as
masculine creatures. This must not be stressed.

Certainly there were many women with the
host. Would they, especially with a woman
commander, remain as camp followers and
spectators? But the last argument is strongest
of all. Suetonius is reported by Tacitus as
telling his legionaries before the final battle,
"There are more women than soldiers in
their ranks." This is a direct statement,
though not necessarily a true one. Whether

there were Amazons in Boadicea's fighting ranks must remain in doubt. But certainly her host was as mixed as it could be, and the administrative problems must have been enormous.

We are not told by what route the host advanced on Colchester, and since we do not know from where it started there is little profit in trying to deduce this. But the tumult of its coming must have given at least a few days' warning to the doomed town. It is difficult to believe that the veterans would not try to throw up some sort of defence in that time. But Tacitus says, "Thwarted by men in the secret of the conspiracy, they dug no trenches and erected no palisades. They omitted to send the old men and women away so as to leave none but young men inside. And having taken no more precautions than in a time of profound peace, they were surrounded by a multitude of barbarians."

With a fifth column among them and an overwhelming force surrounding them the veterans had no chance. The outlying buildings were immediately overrun and burned to the ground. The garrison made their last stand in the Temple of Claudius. There they held out for two days. Then they were overwhelmed and all the inmates slaughtered. It was a ruthless, barbaric massacre.

With the destruction of Colchester and its garrison the emotional objective was achieved. But even if Boadicea wanted to stop there she could not. The IX Legion was stationed at Lincoln, 120 miles away. Its commander had been deceived throughout the weeks of preparation. But he must have known of the march south almost as soon as it began, and he would move fast. At any moment he might attack the host in the disorganization of victory.

Boadicea detached a powerful force to deal with this threat. It cannot have been easy. Facing a legion was a very different task from overrunning an unprotected town. One doubts if she could have got the force moving without leading it herself. In any case she must be given full credit for this tactical move. The Roman historians clearly show resentment that their reverses were suffered at the hands of a woman. Had they been able to point to some man, some mastermind, behind her they would certainly have named him. But no other individual is mentioned at all. The angry mother had become a general.

The direct route for the legion would be Ermine Street as far as Godmanchester and then by the Via Devana through Cambridge. The forces may have met near Godmanchester. Tacitus is laconic. "The victorious Britons went out to meet Petilius Cerialis, Legate of the Legion, who was advancing to the rescue. They routed the legion and slaughtered all his infantry. Cerialis himself escaped with the cavalry, and found shelter behind the defences of his camp." From this one supposes that he was chased all the way back to the Lincoln fortress. The legion later required 2,000 infantry to bring it up to strength. The well-armed and disciplined Romans almost invariably inflicted far more damage than they received, so Boadicea may have lost two or three times as many.

The capture and sacking of Colchester had been of psychological value, but in their second battle her army had won a harder and more militarily important victory. Apart from Suetonius, wherever he might be, there remained no Roman force capable of opposing her in the whole eastern half of Britain.

Now there could be no stopping or going back. Rome never forgot an affront, least of all a military defeat. Neither she nor her people could be safe until every Roman soldier had been killed or driven from Britain.

This consummation suddenly appeared possible. The only serious threat remaining was Suetonius. If he could be eliminated the garrisons of Gloucester, Wroxeter, Chester and the lesser forts could be snuffed out one by one.

It was at this stage of Boadicea's campaign that Suetonius and his cavalry arrived in London. If her thinking had become as military as her behaviour suggests she would be glad of this. He had travelled much faster than expected, therefore his force would be tired. Instead of having to march west and look for him she had him in an indefensible town harassed by thousands of frightened non-combatants. She gathered up her scattered forces and descended on London.

But Suetonius, with all the facts before him, had made his own appreciation. London could not be held with the cavalry alone. His infantry marching from Wales could not arrive in less than a week. Before that Boadicea would probably attack. Therefore he must withdraw. That he would thereby be condemning many thousands of civilians to death made no difference to this military evaluation.

The despair of the townspeople when they saw those whom they had looked upon as their saviours preparing to desert them can easily be imagined. Tacitus puts Suetonius's action in the best light he can. "He decided to save the whole province by the sacrifice of this single town. No tears, no lamentations from those who begged his help could prevent him from giving the signal for departure. Those who could keep up with him were given a place in the column: but all who, because of their sex or age, or love for the place, chose to stay, were butchered by the enemy."

The British horde burst into London on the heels of Suetonius and there was an orgy of slaughter and destruction. Dio goes into details about the outrages perpetrated by the Britons, the skewering of Roman women on long stakes, and more besides. Tacitus is vivid enough. "The Britons were not interested in taking prisoners or selling them as slaves, nor in any of the usual commerce of war," he says, "but only in killing by the sword, the gibbet, by fire and the cross."

It is as if Boadicea was losing control of her enormous and ill-integrated host. Perhaps this entered into the calculations of Suetonius. Once his infantry and baggage train caught up with him he would have a force of about two legions' strength, plus auxiliaries. This would still be far inferior in numbers to the British host, but the morale of his men would not deteriorate. Hers, on the other hand, had no training, no discipline. Still more important, they had no pay. No one who had received the attention of the Procurator had any money left; and they were not, we are told, interested in "the usual commerce of war." A period of inactivity or of fruitless hunting for their chief enemy might tempt many to drift off to their homes.

What the host did was to double back to St. Albans, where the same story of slaughter and destruction was repeated. Recent excavations at Verulamium have disclosed a thick layer of burnt débris which undoubtedly dates from this time. The third Roman town was utterly destroyed. But the military situation had not improved for Boadicea since her defeat of IX Legion. If the revolt was to succeed, Suetonius had to be beaten in battle.

This would have been easier if she had followed him closely as he retreated from London. But if she intended this she did not succeed as she had at Colchester. He had got away, and she did not even know where he was. So the capture of London was in effect a tactical defeat.

VII

THE FINAL BATTLE

The climax of the rebellion was the final battle. One is in a hurry to hear about it and its result. The classical historians were no less impatient to tell of it. Tacitus, having described the sack of London, and given the fearful figure of 70,000 Roman citizens and allies slaughtered there and at Colchester and St. Albans, begins the next paragraph:

"By now Suetonius Paulinus had with him the XIV Legion and a detachment of the XX, together with auxiliary troops from the nearest fort, a total of 10,000 men, and he decided to make an end of delay and seek engagement in battle."

What delay? Tacitus has certainly not delayed. Dio says: "Paulinus... was not willing to risk a conflict with the barbarians immediately, as he feared their numbers and their desperation, but was inclined to delay battle to a more convenient season. But as he grew short of food and the barbarians pressed relentlessly upon him, he was compelled, contrary to his judgement, to engage them."

Here is another mention of delay. There is no hint of how long it lasted. We have to arrive at the duration of the revolt by other means. The tribes had not sown their corn before they went to war. When organized fighting ended they had no crops to harvest. From this one may deduce that the hosting was in March or April and the final battle in July or August—four months at least. Since the first moves were certainly swift it appears that the later manœuvring was protracted. During the final weeks or months the moves of the two sides—the reinforcing, the concentration or dispersal—must have had their effect upon the final result. But nothing has been found to fill this gap in time. The only evidence is of a negative nature. So we must do the best we can by putting ourselves in the place of the two leaders.

Suetonius withdrew from London because he was too weak to face the British host. Where could he go? The north and north-east were swarming with enemies. There was not enough shipping for him to have evacuated from the Thames estuary. But he certainly would not have done this even if it had been possible. Catus had run away by ship—and broken his career thereby. That he was a crook was less venal in Roman eyes than that he was a coward.

Suetonius was certainly not a coward. But he might have withdrawn to the south with the intention of concentrating his forces in Kent and Sussex. There he could have awaited reinforcements from the continent. The Cantiaci were completely under the Roman heel—ever since forty-three baggage trains and columns of reinforcements had been travelling the road from Richborough through Canterbury and Rochester to London. This almost daily exhibition of Roman riches and strength had kept them quiet. And the Regni of Sussex were ruled by Cogidubnus, the most Romanized of all the client kings. He had been rewarded with Roman citizenship and the title *Rex et legatus Augusti in Britannia*. (One may mention in passing that after forty years of faithful service his kingdom was absorbed into the province like all the rest.) In Kent Suetonius would have been safe enough. But it would have been both dangerous and time-consuming for his legions to concentrate there. The IX at Lincoln would have had to pass right through the enemy-occupied territory, but was in no state for fighting its way anywhere. The legions in the west could have joined him with less difficulty. But this would have amounted to throwing away all the conquests of seventeen years without a fight, just because the rebels had overrun three scarcely defended cities. Evacuation, we may be sure, was never in the aggressive mind of Suetonius, unless directly ordered by Rome.

The possibilities remaining open to him were to withdraw to the west or north-west. A hundred miles to the west lay Gloucester and II Legion which was intact as far as we know. Intact, but at the very best untrustworthy since its acting commander had disobeyed a direct order. Every argument favoured the north-west. If he withdrew by the way he had come, within a few days he would fall back on his well-tried infantry, following him from Wales.

We may take it that that is what he did. Possibly he did not leave London by Watling Street, which passed through St. Albans. Even if the British host was still in Essex he would have been too close to it for comfort. He may have put the Thames between himself and Boadicea and made a detour by Staines or even Silchester, thirty miles further on, which was a growing Roman town. If so he must

131

then have doubled back along the line of the
Chilterns to meet the legions, which would in
that case have been halted by galloping
messengers. For meet them he did. Tacitus
says he had with him the XIV and detachments
of the XX legion when he decided to give
battle, and these formations had been with him
in Wales.

Some authorities have doubted whether he
could have made such a manœuvre swiftly
enough to avoid Boadicea with his column
hampered by refugees. But there is no reason
to suppose that he was thus encumbered. The
sentence where Tacitus refers to the people of
London reads, "Those who could keep up
with him were given a place in his column."
Since his column was of cavalry, only fit men
with horses could have kept up with him.
These might be useful. All the rest were left
behind. A general who could abandon a town
of some 25,000 inhabitants to destruction did
so for a good reason, and we may take it that
he was consistent.

Thus we suppose that he met XIV Legion
and a detachment of XX somewhere on Watling
Street. But he needed further reinforcements
and he needed food. At or near High Cross,

24. A highly decorated British dagger of iron with a bronze sheath, similar no doubt to those used by Boadicea's troops. It was found in the Thames River in Berkshire.

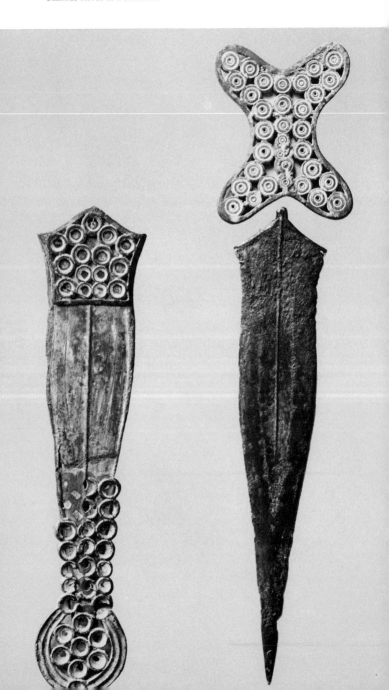

at the junction with the Fosse Way, he would be well placed to gather additional forces from the west or centre of the frontier region. But he could only do this by weakening the forts from which they came. If their strength was too much reduced, the uncommitted tribes would be encouraged to throw in their lot with Boadicea. Thus he would gain reinforcements at the cost of adding considerably to the ranks of the enemy. There were the Brigantes to be considered, the Welsh tribes, and perhaps the Cornovii. According to Tacitus he summoned only "auxiliary troops from the nearest fort."

There remained the question of food for his 10,000 men. The baggage train was following from Wales, but at the end of a campaign it is unlikely that there would be much corn available from that source. It was by this time summer, ten months or so from the last harvest. The supplies of the local Britons would be running low, and they would hide their grain rather than have it commandeered, particularly if they had not sown that spring. But Suetonius could order in a certain amount from the nearest forts. He could do this best if he remained in one place, with good communications in all directions.

When he had gathered enough food, and as many reinforcements as he dared, there would be no advantage in delaying the final battle any longer. So: "He decided to make an end of delay and to seek an engagement."

The suggestion that the final battle was fought on or near Watling Street in the area of High Cross is only acceptable if it fits with the probable, or at least possible, movements of Boadicea. Several authorities, Lewis Spence among them, have suggested that she remained on the northern side of London, somewhere in Epping forest. As a result they place the final battle thereabout—in Essex, or, in the opinion of Spence, the site of Kings Cross station. But the arguments for this depend primarily on the assumption that Suetonius withdrew southwards into Kent or Sussex, which we have discounted. The battle has also been sited as far afield as Chester, by the German scholars Mommsen and Domaszewski. This would be a very long way for Boadicea's ill-organized army to march through a country of unknown and possibly hostile tribes. And it would mean that Suetonius returned almost to his starting point, which hardly fits in with his shortage of food and anxiety to settle the issue.

Boadicea reached London shortly after Suetonius left it. That she failed to follow him closely and bring him to battle before he was reinforced and could choose his own battle-ground, was her first bad military error. The scope and secrecy of the mobilization, the descent on Colchester and quick turn-about to deal with IX Legion were brilliant. So why this failure? As suggested earlier, she might already have begun to lose control of her heterogeneous host. But so early in the campaign, and after nothing but successes, her prestige must have been high, and it is hard to believe that on so important an issue she was thwarted by disobedience alone.

A possible explanation lies in the extent of the early successes, and in Celtic religion. London offered less resistance than Colchester. There was no strongly built temple to hold out against fire and battering ram. But there was more destruction to be done, more killing, and perhaps more sacrifice to the deity held responsible for success. Dio says that the worst atrocities, including the skewering of women on long sharp stakes, were committed in the sacred groves of Andastra. Nowhere else is there mention of this goddess. But it has been pointed out by Dr. Anne Ross that the names of Celtic deities varied from place to place, from Ireland through England to Gaul, although what they stood for was generally the same. Their commonest function was in war and fertility—in other words killing and sex. It is a particularly unpleasant thought that at the dawn of Christianity, when some Christians may already have been in the country, the Britons were practising such revolting religious rites. But it may have been so, and it may well have been this that robbed them of their best chance of winning freedom. The name Andastra has been interpreted as Victory. The Irish Morrigan, Queen of Nightmares, seems more appropriate.

A more acceptable reason for the delay in London might have been the collection of corn from Roman store houses. But it is hard to believe that an old soldier like Suetonius would not have destroyed the remainder after supplying his own men and the inhabitants. Nor does that explanation fit with the subsequent descent on St. Albans where similar enormities—or religious rites—were done.

The sacking of St. Albans is in any case difficult to understand. Colchester and London were Roman towns. Verulamium was certainly Romanized. It was a *municipium*. But it was the capital of the Catuvellauni, many of whom had flocked to the hosting in Icenia and taken their part in the fighting, which should have created an *esprit de corps*. But Verulamium was burnt to the black layer of ashes still to be seen. Was it another sacrifice to Andastra or an act of mere destruction by men and women intoxicated by it and seeking for more? Certain it is that Boadicea went from London not on the trail of Suetonius but to St. Albans.

But after that there was no more to destroy, or not without hard fighting, for apart from tribal centres against which there could be no animosity there remained only the Roman garrisons, all many miles distant. The destruction of Suetonius was the next step. If Boadicea had the clarity of mind which her organizational ability suggests she surely saw this was essential. To her host, which had put IX Legion out of action and frightened Suetonius out of London, this must have appeared quite easy. It was an article of British faith that Caesar had been driven out; Dio puts this thought into Boadicea's rallying speech:

"To speak the plain truth, it is we who have made ourselves responsible for all these evils, in that we allowed them to set foot on the island in the first place instead of expelling them at once as we did their famous Julius Caesar."

The Romans could be beaten and driven out. But where was Suetonius and his army? Boadicea had no intelligence service. Her tribal units knew no more of England than their own districts. They could not have drawn a map even of the southern third of the country. Rumours there would be in plenty, but it would be difficult to evaluate them— as it would have been comparatively easy for Suetonius to arrange for false information to be carried.

Things must have been extraordinarily difficult for Boadicea at this time. An army of tribal units was notoriously brittle. In defeat it splintered and disappeared. In success it was almost as likely to break up and go home with its booty. Inaction was the most dangerous state of all. The Romans had been allowed to land unopposed at Richborough because they did not appear until two months after they were expected, and the temporary British soldiers had gone back to their farms. After the sack of St. Albans there were tasks to be done, reorganization and the collection of food by forage and hunting. But it was no doubt difficult to organize this for the good of the whole host as opposed to that of the foragers and hunters. And there would always be the temptation for a man to slip back to his own land where his presence was so necessary.

Boadicea must have been relieved when at last she had news of Suetonius. It is by no means impossible that he actively enabled her to have this information; for if she did not go and look for him he would have had to hunt for her, which would have prevented him from preparing a position. With numbers so heavily in favour of the British it was essential for him to choose his own ground. However obtained, the information was that the Romans were on Watling Street. The British host trundled off north-westward with their chariots, foot soldiers and family waggons—a column many miles in length.

There would be signs of the Romans all the way along. The scent was hot. The similarity with a hunt and its followers is inescapable. Noisy, cheerful, certain of victory, the Britons swung down the ancient British track which the Romans had paved and straightened out. One pictures the warriors swaggering along, the creaking waggons, the gossiping women,

139

the children, the dogs, the farm animals, the chariots overtaking on the verges.

There was forest then on both sides, but the slopes were of course the same as they are now. Anyone who travels Watling Street must be impressed by its endless undulations... From the next crest the Roman army might come into view... But a hundred miles of marching disclosed only their overnight camps, and litter thrown aside during the marching and counter-marching of the XIV and XX and of the cavalry. These would be welcomed by the British commander for their effect of maintaining the excitement of the chase. There was no need to urge on the tribal units. Rather it was a race between them to be first at the kill.

One wonders if Boadicea ever suspected that she might be being led into a trap. In country so thickly forested, with scant communications, Suetonius could surely have concealed his whereabouts for much longer. Instead there was this straight road which with every milestone told of the Roman troops.

If she thought she was being invited to attack the Governor's force she accepted the challenge. If a trap was intended it was baited by Roman soldiers whom her own force outnumbered. She could not, of course, know the odds with any certainty, but she would be aware of the size Suetonius's force had been in London and feel confident that it had not been increased to any great extent. Confidence was the key to the British mood.

After a hundred miles they reached High Cross. An examination of Watling Street on the London side of that point reveals no place which fits Tacitus's description of the battlefield. That in itself is not proof. But as we have seen, Suetonius probably withdrew to the area of High Cross the better to build up his forces and supplies. Professor Donald Dudley and Dr. Graham Webster have put forward a site some twenty miles further to the northwest, which seems in every way more likely than the various claims of other authorities. Unless something is discovered to discount it, we can accept their suggestion.

High Cross is a lonely place today, windswept and open, with only three or four houses at the junction of Watling Street and the Fosse Way. Then it was forested, with the two straight roads stretching like a great cross as far as the eye could reach between the trees. There was a small Roman post which would certainly have been evacuated and destroyed by its garrison. Possibly the ashes were still warm.

From there Watling Street led on in long and gentle undulations, but never overlooked by higher ground on either side for a distance of twenty miles. Then there is a slight rise which stretches obliquely across the line of the road, and is indented by defiles. It is composed of older, igneous rocks on which a different vegetation would grow. It rises only some two hundred feet. But it provides a vantage ground above Watling Street.

The brief description of the battlefield given by Tacitus is as follows: "He [Suetonius] chose a position in a narrow defile, protected from behind by forest. Here he could be sure that there would be no enemy except in front, where an open plain gave no cover for ambushes."

It is not easy to picture the scene as it was nineteen hundred years ago, even if the choice of site is correct. The suggested place is near to the present village of Mancetter (the Roman Manduessedum) which lies between Caldecote, north of Nuneaton, and Atherstone. The imaginative eye must first sweep away hundreds of modern houses and an industrial estate and then clothe the ground with its original vegetation.

The Roman commander had chosen the place with care so that his 10,000 could not be outflanked or surrounded by the 50,000 or more British warriors. The defile sloped up into the ridge and was weathered out into the shape of the bow of an open boat beached on a sand bank. The ridge was forested, not with big, widely-set trees but with the thicker-growing and more stunted sorts which survive in an exposed position—elder, thorn, holly, and briars. This also clad the forward side of the ridge, but we can deduce that the defile itself was open. Also in front there was a wide clear space on a soil of sand and gravel which ran down to the road and over it until big trees rose again in the heavy marl beyond.

The first contact which the Britons made would be with outposts on the road some miles in front of the position. Their duty was to gallop back and give warning. One can well imagine the excited shout of tens of thousands of voices at this unmistakeable sign that the clash was near.

Then the Roman army itself came in view a mile or two in front. We have from Tacitus an exact description of how the force was disposed, and a skeletal account of the battle itself. Tacitus was a specialist in battle descriptions, writing for a connoisseur public. The Roman army fought to exact patterns,

with well-defined drill and manœuvres. For
Tacitus it was only necessary to announce the
type of battle (like a gambit in chess), and
describe anything unusual or dramatic which
resulted; the rest would be understood by
Romans brought up on their history of war.
So we may be justified, on the basis of other
battles, in describing this one in more detail
than he did. It was, as it turned out, a text-
book encounter between a small, well-drilled
force on ground of their own choosing and
a huge barbarian horde.

When the advancing British column first
saw the Roman army it was drawn up in line
across the defile. The Roman legionaries were
in the centre, probably six ranks deep. On
either side of them were the auxiliaries, men not
Italian-born but trained in the same thorough
way; and the cavalry were on the wings. The
whole line was scarcely a thousand yards across.

The British host poured off the road and
spread out on the open flat. They could have
made a line far more extensive than that of the
Romans, but the defile restricted them to the
same frontage for attack. There was procedure
of honour in forming centre, right or left. This
would take time to work out even though the
orders were already agreed.

25. A fine tombstone portrait of Marcus Facilis, found at Colchester. He was a centurion of the XX Legion, which fought with Suetonius against Boadicea's hordes. He wears the regulation sword and dagger and holds a staff of vine wood in his right hand, symbol of his rank.

26. An antefix, or roof decoration made of pottery, showing the name and symbols of the XX Legion which fought with Suetonius in the final, dreadful battle against Boadicea, in which some 80 000 Britons were said to have perished.

The interval while the two armies were facing up to each other, still far out of range, was the time when the commanders gave their orders and exhortations. The history of antiquity is spiced by these harangues, and the reader may have wondered how an army spread over half a square mile could hear. The answer is that they could not, and in fact the recorded speeches probably derive more from the imagination of the historians than the mouths of the generals. But orders at least had to be heard. The Roman custom was to call the unit commanders together to hear the General's plan and exhortation, then dismiss them to their units to pass on the essence. This scarcely differs from present-day custom— except that modern generals reserve their eloquence until they write their memoirs.

Suetonius is credited by Tacitus with a short speech—which Agricola, as a staff officer, would have heard.

"Pay no attention to the noise these savages make. Ignore their empty threats. There are more women than soldiers in their ranks. They are not warlike and they are badly armed. When they experience the weapons and courage of troops who have often beaten them before, they will turn and run. In an army of many

legions, few win battle honours. What glory
will be yours, a small band which fights for
the honour of the whole army! Keep your
ranks. Throw your javelins. Strike with your
shield bosses. Then drive on. Do not pause
for booty. Win the battle and you win it all."

Boadicea is also said to have addressed her
followers, though how her words could have
been recorded it is hard to know. In any case
few of the host could have heard her, for the
Britons were notoriously noisy when the
intoxication of battle gripped them—blowing
their horns, clashing sword on shield, shouting
war cries. She visited each tribal unit,
proclaiming that although their people were
accustomed to the leadership of women in
battle, she was among them not as a royal
person but as a woman fighting for freedom,
to avenge the bruising of her body and the
rape of her daughters. The gods would grant
this vengeance. The Romans would never
face the roar and din of the British thousands,
still less their charge and hand-to-hand attack.
Numbers were on their side, justice was on
their side. It was victory or death. As a
woman she was resolved not to live as a slave.
The men could do as they liked.

It was exhortation, not orders. The men

cheered wildly. Those who could not hear her saw her driving round in her chariot in her striking clothes, her long hair flying. Her two daughters were with her, by their presence conveying her message even without words.

Such battles opened with the swift manœuvres of skirmishers between the hosts. The auxiliaries on the Roman side, recruited from Spain, the Pyrenees, Gaul, Thrace and Germany, were allowed to keep their traditional weapons. So there were archers, both mounted and on foot, slingers, cavalry, spearmen. They harassed the enemy units while they were forming up, sling bolts and arrows flying. With the British this task of disorganization belonged chiefly to the charioteers. They had bowmen too, but the British archers had not yet won renown.

This was only the curtain raiser. When the last arrow and sling bolt had flown, the auxiliaries fell back precipitately before the main encounter. For the Celts the encounter was the charge. It was almost the whole gamble of the battle, a rush of such wild impetuosity that it often settled the issue within minutes.

No doubt on this occasion it would have been wiser to use their advantage in numbers more circumspectly. Only a force equal to that of the Romans could actually oppose them in a charge because there was room for no more on that narrow front. But others, before the charge, could have infiltrated on either side of the defile, worked their way through the thick woodland and caused a lot of trouble on the flanks and at the rear.

The Britons were too impatient for such tactics, too certain of success. They charged in a solid mass, the tribal leaders in front and their men behind them. By all accounts the noble Celt was a splendid figure, tall, athletic, bearded and with long hair, fair or auburn. They towered over the stubby little legionaries, and they came on with all the clamour of war cry and trumpet. They were handicapped by charging up hill, but they came on recklessly. When running at full speed it is more natural for a man to hold his arms wide rather than cover his body with shield and weapon.

The legionaries were in line, five or six ranks deep. When the enemy were forty yards distant the front rank threw the first light javelin. Each man then immediately reached behind him and to the right, took the second javelin from his companion in the second rank and threw that close behind the first. That done, the drill was for the front rank to side-step and fall back while the second rank repeated the throw, either with light javelin or heavy, according to the range. This was repeated with the quickness born of long and careful practice until the enemy were within ten yards or so.

It does not take charging men many seconds to cover thirty yards—not if they have a clear run and do not check. The Britons were charging up a slope. Many of their leaders must have been transfixed by the first javelin volley, more by the second, more by the third and fourth. Those who had opposed their shields in time would be struggling with seven-foot shafts. The men behind could only continue their advance by pushing past them or jumping over the dead. It is a shock to see a man skewered right through, writhing like a worm on a hook. It would be only natural if the bravest checked for a moment.

In this moment, at trumpet blast order, the legionaries closed ranks, raised their long shields, drew their short broad swords and shuffled forward down the slope in wedge formation. To achieve this wedge one century went in front, two others following in echelon, a fourth in reserve to plug any gap or reinforce success. The units might be larger than the century—a cohort in a large army. But that was the principle. The effect was a series of wedges which hammered into the enemy mass. Hammer is the apt word, for the shield boss was used with the force of a trotting man behind it. His left arm punched with the shield while the sword in his right hand stabbed like a serpent's tongue.

The enemy, out of breath and shocked by the javelin volleys, were generally divided by the wedges into triangular shaped groups of men who suddenly found it necessary to fight on two fronts. This was demoralizing.

The Celts were by this time fighting hand to hand in a general mêlée which left little room for manœuvre. No man however strong can fight with the energy of a boxer for more than a minute or two without gravely deteriorating in skill through weariness. In single combat the opponents tire and deteriorate together. But another item of Roman battle drill, similar to that of javelin throwing, was for the front rank swordsman to side-step and fall back to the rear, leaving the man behind him to take his place. Therefore the Briton was faced by a fresh opponent.

Each Roman had to kill five or more Britons to win. But they worked in shifts, cutting through the leaders to the men behind. In a tightly-fought battle it only needs a break in one place to cause the beginning of a rout. When hard-pressed men know that something has gone wrong and cannot see what it is, fear quickly turns to panic.

The *alae* of cavalry, the élite of the army, were on the wings waiting for this break. A good general was quick to see the chance when it came, and to order a charge with lances. There was a scream of trumpets and a thunder of hooves from both sides. The British mass, wedged into in front, pierced from the best men to the worst, and now charged upon with all the impetuosity of a downhill gallop from the flanks, broke and fled.

But they could not retreat far. This battle had as macabre an ending as it is possible to imagine. The waggons full of women and children, the families of the warriors, had been drawn up as closely together as they could be parked near the foot of the defile to watch their menfolk win their final victory. They blocked the line of retreat. The running men were crowded in a helpless, seething throng against the waggons. The terror of mass hysteria is well known to us from crowd accidents when no enemy is about. With attacking Romans stabbing their way on one side, women and children shrieking on the other, the horror is fortunately beyond the scope of our experience.

Steadily, inexorably, the legionaries and auxiliaries butchered their way through to the waggons. They climbed over these on the piles of dead, killing the women and children and the draught animals. The cavalry raced after those who had managed to escape from the shambles of the waggon park, cutting them down.

Tacitus wrote. "It was a glorious victory, like those of the good old days. Some estimate as many as 80,000 British dead. There were only 400 Romans killed, and scarcely more wounded."

VIII

THE PAX ROMANA

Boadicea's last battle resulted in the greatest slaughter this island has ever known. Tacitus suggests that it was all over in a matter of hours. The casualty figure he gives is the same as that for Hiroshima in 1945 when the first atomic bomb was dropped. In both cases, of course, women and children were included as well as combatants. The difference is in the duration of the killing, hours as opposed to seconds, and to the fact that Hiroshima, with Nagasaki following, brought the end of that war. In Britain in the year 60 the battle marked the beginning of a much wider destruction by sword, hunger, exposure and disease which obliterated many more people. Exact figures are impossible to arrive at. But if one is right in estimating that the whole British population amounted to half a million—as opposed to fifty million now—the resultant shock of casualties would, mathematically, be a hundred times as great. Without stressing an un-satisfactory type of argument one may make the point that Boadicea's revolt and its aftermath caused an upheaval and destruction of maximum significance.

It was remarked earlier that Suetonius must have hated Boadicea for turning upside down his victory in Wales. Through her he hated all her people. The policy he adopted during the remainder of his governorship went far beyond punitive repression. He seemed vindictively determined upon the annihilation of whole sections of the British community—the Iceni and Trinovantes, at least—and on the most harsh suppression of other tribes.

Tacitus says in the *Annals*: "The whole army was concentrated and kept in tents to finish the war.... The territory of all tribes that had been hostile or neutral was laid waste with fire and sword."

It was not enough to have refrained from joining the rising. To have fallen short of active support of the Roman side was a crime. Order had been re-established before winter came, but the killing went on. There is a significant passage in the *Agricola*. "The issue of a single battle restored it [Britain] to its old obedience. Even so, many of the rebels remained under arms, very conscious of their disloyalty, and naturally apprehensive about the

Governor, fearing that—however admirable in other respects—he might act harshly to those who surrendered and pursue a cruel policy, for he was a man who avenged every wrong done to him."

The Trinovantes, placed as they were within the road system of the three towns, had no more chance than rabbits in a hayfield with reapers scything towards them from all sides. The Iceni, scattered throughout their forested and marshy country, and with no villages or towns of any size, were harder to hunt down. Many no doubt were killed that autumn or rounded up and sent as slaves to the mines of Britain, or by chain gang to Rome. But the operation was not completed that winter. The elusiveness of the Iceni is remarkable, for Tacitus's phrase, "the whole army was concentrated," must mean that very large forces were used in the hunt.

The wooden houses were quickly found and burned, the farm animals slaughtered or driven off. The people too old or too young to move were treated according to the mood of the hunters or the orders they had received. The rest took to the forest. There they were hunted like vermin. For soldiers from warmer, drier lands to live under canvas instead of in the comparative comfort of winter quarters was already a hardship. One pictures the sullen, sodden men searching through wet woods.

If it was hard on the hunters, how was it for the hunted? They had no roof, no warmth, no safety, no future. And they had no food except for the little they could hunt while being hunted. That spring "they had omitted to sow the crops and brought every man into the army."

If they had sown they would have been granted no chance to reap. So perhaps it made no difference. But the result was famine. Few people in our civilization have experienced real hunger. The present writer happens to have done so at sub-zero temperatures and feels justified in obtruding himself to mention one result. It subordinates all the better feelings, leaving only the most primitive and selfish. Here they would feel hate for their well-fed hunters. What else was there to feel except their hunger pangs?

The hunters, cold and resentful at their winter task, felt equal hatred. Some of them had seen the skewered Roman women at Londinium, and the atrocities at the other two towns. The rest had heard of them. The men they were actually hunting might not have been responsible, but they were of the same race. It was hatred to the death of one race for another.

As for the personal hate of Suetonius for Boadicea, that was thwarted because she was dead. She and her daughters disappeared from the eyes of the Romans, and from history, after the chariot drive through her ranks before the battle. We do not even know her daughters' names. Apparently the Queen got back to her own country, and there died—Dio says from a disease and Tacitus by taking poison. Perhaps the latter is the more acceptable end. She had nothing more to live for, only to be marched in chains in a Roman triumph before execution. Certainly she could do nothing for her people. But if she thought that by eliminating herself she might reduce the retribution she was wrong. The killing continued into the spring. When the hunters could not find the men and women they destroyed the means by which they lived, which came to the same thing in the end. There can have been little more sowing in the spring of 61 than there had been in 60. Dr. Godwin's paper on *Pollen-Analytic Evidence,* quoted in the second chapter, states, "The Romanisation of Norfolk was tardy and less intense than in other areas of Britain, possibly because the Early Roman period was marked by the abortive revolt of the Iceni under Boudicca and its subsequent cruel repression."

Let us look at the situation for a moment from the Roman viewpoint. The prime intention of making the province pay was further than ever from being realized. There was no lack of slave labour for the mines, of course. But this was only one source of revenue, and a comparatively small one, for the north Midlands had not yet been reached, while the extreme west of Cornwall with its tin, and Wales with copper and gold, were still unpacified. For the rest, you cannot extract taxes from people whom you kill or drive into the woods.

The state of Britain was the more chaotic because Procurator Catus when he ran away had taken with him all his staff and most of the records. The rest had been destroyed in the flames of the revolt. When a new procurator was sent to fill the vacancy, before the end of the year 60, he had to start from the beginning— in a province seventeen years old.

It will be as well to remind ourselves of a procurator's function and powers. He was the head of the civil service and treasury in the country. Being of slightly lower status than the governor he could not act against his orders, but he had the right to report directly to the Emperor, and to put forward his own recommendations. Catus had acted during the absence of Suetonius in Wales, and therefore not directly against orders, but rather as a deputy on his own authority. The interest of Suetonius was now mainly concentrated on East Anglia, and we may suppose that he never left it for long. A great deal would therefore depend upon the character of the new Procurator and how he and the governor got on together, for they would be working together, seeing each other almost every day.

The new Procurator, Julius Alpinus Classicianus, was not a Roman. He came from Trier—Trèves on the Moselle—a place which, incidentally, contains the most remarkable Roman remains of any town in northern Europe. Professor Birley has proved that he must have obtained Roman citizenship at least twenty years earlier. But since by birth and upbringing he belonged to a province he was not blinded by imperial prejudice against the British. He was middle-aged, perhaps in later middle age, married, with one daughter. He has come down to us as a man of absolute integrity and great moral courage.

He and Suetonius did not work well together. Suetonius was honest. It had become all too common for a governor to make money out of his province, but it is certain that Suetonius did not make a denarius out of Britain. Class difference, if it had existed as it did with Catus, would have been less apparent, since he and the Procurator were of different nations; but in any case Classicianus was of a noble family. He and the governor were both educated and intelligent men. But their points of view were diametrically opposed.

Suetonius had proved himself an Ancient Roman in the way he had refused to accept defeat, had faced up to odds of five or more to one, and conquered. The Ancient Roman had faults as well as virtues. With courage and determination went lack of imagination. Kindly feelings were to be subordinated in oneself and ignored in others. Pride was admirable. So was revenge—which should be far more severe than the damage received. Suetonius continued his policy of ruthless destruction. The approach of summer made the task less uncomfortable and more rapid.

Classicianus was totally opposed to this. Whether he had sympathy for the Iceni and the other rebel tribes we do not know, but he

pointed out the difference between destruction
and construction as it affected revenue. Suetonius would not listen. The harrying
continued. Classicianus had no power to stop
it, but he wrote direct to the Emperor saying
that matters could never be bettered until the
governor was replaced.

Tacitus strongly disapproved of this behaviour. Classicianus, he says, "allowed his
private quarrels to obstruct the public interest,
stating that it would be wise to wait for a new
governor who, lacking the hate of an enemy
or the arrogance of a conqueror, would be
inclined to show mercy to those who
surrendered."

One may be sure that the new Procurator
was unpopular in all Roman circles in Britain.
He had not seen the horror of the rebellion,
and here he was advocating mildness. But
Classicianus was as obstinate as Suetonius.
He continued to speak his mind and to write
on the same theme to the Emperor.

Nero did not at once commit himself. He
was twenty-three years old and less interested
in government than in his pleasures. The
Terror of his later years had not yet begun and
he still retained his old counsellors, Burrhus
and Seneca. This was a difficult matter for them

to advise on. The argument of Classicianus could not be ignored, for it was borne out by the finances of Britain. Everything pointed to the advisability of a change of policy. But not, for other reasons, to a change of governor. Militarily, Suetonius had done brilliantly. Both with the legions in Britain and the public in Rome his prestige was very high indeed. To recall him before the end of his governorship would cause an outcry if nothing worse. Also there was the possibility that Classicianus was wrong. Another and totally unbiassed opinion was needed. Therefore it was decided to send out a commission of enquiry.

Meanwhile the campaign—for it was no less than that—against the remnants of the rebels continued. There may still have been bands at large in the Midland forest. There was certainly a hard core in Norfolk. It would be fascinating to know how and where they held out. Professor Dudley and Dr. Graham Webster speak of excavations at Thornham, on the Norfolk corner of the Wash, which suggest that the Iceni made a last stand there. Another possibility is the Fens, where Hereward the Wake retained his freedom as an outlaw almost exactly a thousand years later. In this stubborn resistance of the Iceni there lies more courage than in the whole rebellion. It has been suggested that it was inspired by the hope of a more lenient governor being appointed. In the quotation from Tacitus given above, Classicianus is in fact held responsible. But it is hard to see how these lonely men and women who lived among reeds or thorny undergrowth could have known what was being discussed in the high places of the enemy. A simpler explanation is more plausible—that they were the sort who do not give in.

While they continued their extraordinarily uncomfortable existence the commission of enquiry was getting under way. It was headed by Polyclitus, secretary to the Emperor. A confidant of Nero was naturally a person of the highest dignity and importance. We may safely presume that he was also a voluptuary. Polyclitus travelled through Italy and Gaul very slowly and with an enormous staff, clerical and household.

He was a freedman. It will be remembered that when Claudius's invasion force refused to embark at Boulogne the freedman Narcissus had been sent for and had talked the legionaries round. Since then freed slaves had been increasingly employed. That a man had risen from less than nothing to the highest rank proved his intelligence and personality. But a freedman had another, and special, value for an emperor. He was unpopular with every class of Roman society—aristocrat, soldier, civil servant, business man—and therefore could be presumed to be impartial. His only loyalty was to the Emperor who had given him his freedom. It was a curious situation. After the terrible convulsion of Boadicea's revolt, and the hundred thousand deaths that had resulted, the fate of Britain was to be adjudged by a man who had been a slave.

The reader must have felt the gaps in this story. The writer has longed for the freedom of fiction to fill them by imagination. What sort of man was this ex-slave sent to give judgement on the treatment of Britain? We shall never know, for character is not a thing dug up by archaeologists; nor was Polyclitus important enough in the Roman Empire to have left a memorial. George Shipway, who recently wrote a very good novel, *Imperial Governor*, about Britain in the years 58-61, gives a convincing sketch of him. He describes Polyclitus at the end of his tour of inspection as going to the slave market and choosing twelve beautiful Trinovantine boys and twelve girls—as one might buy souvenirs to take home.

It is history that Polyclitus made a thorough tour of inspection. The deference shown to him by both the military and civil side of the Roman administration puzzled and possibly amused the British, who knew that he had been a slave. They surely deserved that small diversion.

The report submitted to Nero by Polyclitus recommended that the policy of attrition be changed to one of conciliation and re-construction. Suetonius, proud and certain of his own rightness, refused to be deflected from his course of vengeance. Fifty thousand soldiers were behind the victorious general. He was a force to be reckoned with.

He was finally recalled in the summer of 61 in connection with the loss of a number of ships and their crews. We are told no more than this. But we know that he was impatiently concerned with wiping out the last pockets of Icenian resistance, and one cannot help supposing that he had used the fleet as he had used it in the Welsh campaign for a combined operation. He went quietly back to Rome, neither as a triumphant general nor in disgrace.

He was once more made consul. The awkward old soldier was allowed to fade away.

Thus, undramatically, the two main figures in this historical episode have disappeared. Life in Britain went on without them. Our final interest is in the revised policy which was adopted as a result of the rebellion. To put it another way, did Boadicea's revolt bring about anything that was good?

Great care was taken in the choice of men to govern Britain, and by them of subordinates for positions of authority over the native people. Rome digested the lesson that human feelings matter, and that rule by force alone is a barren policy.

The successor of Suetonius was Petronius Turpilianus, who was governor for three years; and although we know little of him apart from the grudging praise of Tacitus that he was "more kindly disposed towards repentance" and "settled the former disorders" without attempting anything further, it is clear that he put an end to the killing—which resulted in the cessation of armed resistance. The stout-hearted remnants of the Iceni could come out of hiding and rebuild their farms. So peaceful in fact did Britain become in this short period that Rome felt able to appoint as

27-28. A reconstruction of Roman Colchester, as it may have looked when rebuilt after Boadicea's destruction of the city, shows the restored Temple of Claudius at its center. The original city had no walls. The Temple, whose foundations have been identified, is shown in a suggested restoration. It was an exceptionally impressive structure for the provinces.

29 -30. London may have looked like this in 50 A.D. before Boadicea destroyed it. After the revolt it became the capital of Roman Britain in place of Colchester. Watling Street, one of the principal Roman roads, led west from London and is still in use today as in the photograph. Suetonius retreated along it towards the final battle against Boadicea.

the next governor a man with no military experience at all. Trebellius Maximus was popular with the Britons but had considerable trouble with the legions which were always most difficult to handle when they had nothing to do.

Under these two governors the foundations of peace and prosperity were laid in Roman-occupied Britain. But credit for the initiation of this better way of life must be given to Classicianus. If he had not made a bold stand against Suetonius—who cannot have been a pleasant man to oppose—things would have gone on as before for some time longer at least. As things worked out, once the change of policy had been made it was the Procurator's duty to implement and oversee the details of the new administration. Classicianus inherited from Catus a tradition of corruption, peculation and downright vice. He built up a civil service of probity and justice. It was his seemingly impossible task to get tribute out of people and also to win their good will. If dead men cannot pay taxes, neither can those who are bankrupt. Classicianus must have possessed humanity, patience and imagination. He should be the patron saint of the Inland Revenue.

It is curious and satisfactory that although we know so little about him personally, except by implication, we have his memorial. His tombstone is in the British Museum. One broken part of it was found on Tower Hill in 1852. This massive piece of stone had been used in strengthening the Roman city wall. It was not generally accepted for what it was until another find which fitted to it put its identification beyond doubt by adding enough to the inscription to make it understandable. This second large fragment was unearthed in 1935. It includes the name of the daughter of Classicianus, Placata, which means Peace.

While still concerned with personalities, we may mention two minor characters of the main story who had a continuing influence in Britain. Both Petilius Cerialis, Legate of IX Legion which was so roughly handled by Boadicea's forces, and Gaius Julius Agricola, the staff officer, became governors of the province.

Cerialis carried the border at least as far as York, setting up a camp there which became the base for all subsequent operations in the north.

The ambition of Agricola was no less than the conquest of all Britain. He went a long way towards achieving it, defeating the Caledonians at Mons Graupius—whatever that name may be in Gaelic. He was recalled before he put to the test his final plans for conquering Scotland. Tacitus paints his military achievements in glowing colours. He is equally laudatory about the advances Agricola made in the more peaceful fields of life.

Authorities are generally agreed that Tacitus over-praised his father-in-law, giving him credit which belongs more rightly to his predecessors. We may, however, cover the developments of the quarter century following the rebellion without ascribing credit to any individual, for this was Romanization, the process applied to every province once it became militarily secure.

Peace was the first essential. That achieved, attention could be given to encouraging the form of life characteristic of Roman civilization. It might be supposed that the first change was towards centralization in towns as opposed to the numerous small tribal settlements. This was Roman policy, as contributing to a better control of the country than existed under a multiplicity of local leaders; and perhaps the growth of towns was the first visible sign. But before that the people had to be educated to accept the change. Colchester, the showpiece town of Camulodunum, failed—apart from the abuses which led to violence—because the whole idea of such a place was inimical to the Celtic point of view. So the nobles were encouraged to send their sons to Roman schools. When they learned to appreciate the Roman conception of civic responsibility, government, recreation, domestic comfort, then they were helped by Roman planners and architects, and possibly by grants of money, to build a town with comfortable houses, forum, theatre, temple and so on. In a town so established the rich citizens vied with each other in providing amenities and in the various forms of public service. But in Caistor-by-Norwich, the Icenian post-rebellion capital, building and development were particularly slow because there were no rich families left.

London on the other hand grew rapidly from its own ashes. It became the capital city, displacing Colchester. The Governor and Procurator had their headquarters there. Nothing could keep London down for long. It had to grow and spread. But the new London was not a ramshackle collection of buildings as the first had been. It was a planned city, well laid out and walled.

In the country Roman forms of building were soon established because they provided a house more convenient and comfortable than the native type. It is a mistake to think of Roman villas as the houses of rich Romans. Most developed from British farms as the native farmers became more prosperous and were imbued, almost imperceptibly, with Roman ideas. The face of the country changed little and slowly, but the straight roads stretched further, connecting the towns which grew up from trading marts about the camps or in places geographically suitable for trade.

According to Strabo, the main British exports at the beginning of the century had been corn, cattle, hides, hunting dogs and slaves. To these were added an increasing quantity of metals as the mines were developed. There were lead ores in many parts of the country, and from these silver was extracted by the smelting process known as cupellation. Iron, tin and copper were also mined, and gold in Carmarthenshire. Coal was also mined, but the only actual record of its use was on the altar of Minerva at Bath.

Ornaments were made from the shale of the Isle of Purbeck and from the jet of the Whitby Lias. British pearls were also popular, though perhaps less so than the oysters themselves. Their shells are dug up in large quantities on the site of almost every military camp. Professor I. A. Richmond suggests that the oyster tavern was the Roman soldier's equivalent of the fish-and-chips shop.

Three breeds of dog are known to have been exported, the Irish wolf hound, the bulldog and the spaniel, while the greyhound is depicted in pottery. Both sealskins and bearskins were used in trade, live bears also being sent to the arenas. Professor Richmond mentions their use for lacerating criminals. The *pax Romana* was not in every sense benign. Cloth from British wool was a valuable product, the most popular abroad being the *birrus Britannicus,* which was waterproof.

Perhaps the most lasting change was in speech. At first Latin was only the official language, spoken when Roman and Briton were concerned together in government, justice, military and civil questions. But it was the only written language, and therefore all who would write must learn it. It spread downwards from the upper levels of society. It spread upwards too—the vulgar Latin of the legionaries and the traders—from their contact with the local people. Since the native

172

tongue was also spoken there was a period of bilingualism.

Latin unquestionably gave a great deal to the language. Take away from modern English every word of Latin derivation and see what is left! Latin was the most concise and precise of the ancient languages. There were many other linguistic influences in this country later—Norman, Saxon, and so on— but the result is that English is as precise as any living tongue and is at the same time the ideal language of poetry. It is interesting, if not paradoxical, that the Scottish, who for geographical reasons were slow to be affected by any foreign influence, speak the best English. The Welsh, still more resistant, kept the Celtic tongue with the addition of a few hundred Latin loan words.

It would be beyond the scope of this book to deal in more detail with the effects of Romanization, or carry the story further. In conclusion we need an assessment of Boadicea for good or ill and of where she stands as a character in our history.

If she had beaten Suetonius in the last battle the Romans would almost certainly have been compelled to evacuate the island. Very likely they would have come back. Britain was not only a potentially valuable province but also a strategic base of great importance. But supposing they had gone for good, would Britain have been the gainer or the loser?

Rome had in the year 60 given only from her worse side—aggressive, cruel, subjugating. What she had to offer in culture, administration, standard of living, came later; and so it would have been missed or at least postponed, as it was for the countries she never visited—such as Scandinavia. Put another way, Rome was a civilization, Britain a collection of barbaric tribes. The influence of Rome must have been progressive.

If so it would seem that Boadicea was a retrogressive influence. She slowed down Romanization—at enormous cost; as in effect though not by intention she made it more humane and considerate. But even if one grants her this, she did not alter the course of history.

She struck the spark which lit the fire. She struck when it was both courageous and right to strike. But she could not, or at any rate did not, control the fire it caused.

She is remembered chiefly through tradition, which takes little account of facts. She is a national figure, more substantial than Britannia

174

because she was a real woman. Tradition has snatched out of the fire she lit one brand which gives only an inspiring light—resistance against oppression and wrong. For that she is rightly remembered. But her voice is the last fierce cry of something old and savage rather than the first expression of noble feeling; and as such, without straining after romanticism, it should be heard.

IX

WHAT REMAINS
TO BE SEEN

The evil that men do lives after them,
The good is oft interred with their bones.

The funeral speech of Mark Antony in Shakespeare's *Julius Caesar* was intended to rouse sympathy for the dead; the speaker is not presented as essentially sincere. But the lines are appropriate for the Queen of the Iceni. She reacted in a way which was originally right. Perhaps the good was later blotted out by evil—interred in an unknown grave.

Certainly she does not appear well in archaeology. All she has left is a layer of ashes. Visually recorded are the good works of the Romans in stone, brick, statuary, inscription, ornament; their cruelties and callousness are gone without trace. That being understood, let us see what remains to be seen of the time of Boadicea.

One can get a strong feeling of the past by visiting the scenes of her destruction. This is less so in London than elsewhere. London is

176

so large. So much else has happened there, so much has been built. In fact the archaeologist has to act quickly if he is to read anything from a foundation site before it is covered by another building. And what has been found can be seen only in the museum. But the relics there leave a vivid impression. There are, for instance, seventeen coins of the reign of Claudius which were in the stratum of ash seventeen feet below Lombard Street. They are partly fused together. The heat was so intense that the natural clay below them was reduced to powder.

London, of course, has known many fires. But those which can be dated by coins, pottery or glass give an indication of the lay-out of the municipium in 60 A.D. It was within the present city limits, north of London Bridge, but straggled out along the high roads to north and west.

In Colchester you see the past around you in the street—the Roman walls with present-day houses and shops built against them and on them. The town walls, of course, were constructed after the disaster, to make sure that the same thing could not happen again. They were built so strongly that, some fourteen hundred years later, they withstood a long siege and cannon fire during Cromwell's rebellion.

The durability of everything the Romans did makes one feel that such people would have come back even if Boadicea had driven them out of Britain. Whatever they set up was meant to last for ever. One feels this in the "vaults" which pass through the foundations both of the Temple of Claudius and of the Castle which the Normans built upon the site. The original temple, though for worship and not defence, was strong enough to hold out for two days until the tens of thousands of besiegers burnt it over the heads of the people inside. One can imagine it being almost covered with firewood to make an immense bonfire.

The temple was certainly built again. The Normans pulled it down and used the stones to build their castle—which is what remains above ground level today. But in the late seventeenth century an attempt was made to pull *it* down as a source of building material. In the course of this semi-demolition a tunnel was driven under the castle, the walls of which are about twenty-five feet thick. Passing through the tunnel, known as the vaults, one sees a section of both the Norman and Roman temple foundations. Both are of concrete. If scratched with a piece of blunt metal, a key or a coin, the Norman concrete comes off in powder. The Roman is hard as stone.

What remains of the castle contains the museum. Here one sees objects of everyday life which were being used in 60 A.D. Most moving are a child's toys made of terra-cotta— a pig, a monkey, a rabbit. And there is a glass feeding bottle for a baby. Such fragile objects have survived even better than metal, which has been corroded.

Excavations have disclosed a similar layer of ash to that found in London. There is besides a tombstone which conveys the destructive rage of the attackers. The stone is carved to depict an auxiliary cavalryman riding his horse over the body of a naked Briton. The figure of the Briton is untouched. So is the inscription, which would have meant nothing to Boadicea's warriors. But the face of the cavalryman has been smashed off.

There is also the cast of a head of the Emperor Claudius which was fished out of the River Alde in 1907. It is deduced that the original, now in the British Museum, had been hacked from a statue, and later thrown away—probably at the time of the persecution, to get rid of the evidence. The man who found it, when he was a boy, is still about. He received five shillings for it. It was recently sold for over £50,000.

The Catuvellauni of Hertfordshire had experience of the Romans more than a century before the time of the rebellion. The fortress of Cassivellaunus which Julius Caesar captured was at Wheathampstead, six miles north of St. Albans. The Belgic tribe then moved to the slopes above the River Ver where the first town of Verulamium was built. From the first there was Roman influence in layout, drainage, type of building, and very likely also in dress and food. It was this collaboration which made the place an object of hatred to Boadicea's people. They burnt it to ashes although, as has recently been shown, it possessed defensive earth works.

The second town plan was completed during the governorship of Agricola. Thereafter Verulamium continued to develop throughout the centuries of Roman occupation. Then the first English saint, Alban, who was executed by the Romans, gave it its present name.

The excavations have been brilliantly carried out. The ruins of this comfortable and important Roman town are there to see—

theatre, hypocaust, beautiful mosaics. But once again the only relic of Boadicea is a layer of ashes.

There is still a great deal to be learned. Boadicea's grave will probably never be found, but the site of the final battle may be exactly fixed. Work continues along Watling Street, and also in the land of the Iceni. "Archaeological excavation," Dr. Graham Webster wrote in 1962, "has over the last few decades become a very precise operation, carried out with the delicate skill of a surgeon and interpreted with the stiff logic of a scientist." During the lifetime of some of us the main gaps in the story of Boadicea are likely to be filled.

HISTORICAL APPENDIX

CHRONOLOGY

	EVENTS IN BRITAIN	EVENTS IN ROME AND THE EMPIRE
B.C. 55	Caesar makes a reconnaissance and returns to Gaul.	Reforms of Crassus and Pompey. Caesar bridges the Rhine.
54	Caesar invades Kent: defeats Cassivellaunus, retires to Gaul. Celtic chieftains regain power.	Break-up of First Triumvirate begins with death of Julia.
51		Publication of Caesar's *Commentarii de Bello Gallico*.
B.C. 30 to A.D. 14	Transference of power from Trinovantes to Catuvellauni.	Reign of Augustus.
A.D. 43	Roman expeditionary force under Aulus Plautius lands at Richborough; Caractacus defeated at Medway. Emperor Claudius occupies Colchester.	Claudius (accession 41 A.D.) decides on invasion of Britain.
47	Ostorius Scapula moves against Caractacus, leader of the Silures.	Claudius revives censorship and the famous secular games.

	EVENTS IN BRITAIN	EVENTS IN ROME AND THE EMPIRE
51	Caractacus seeks refuge with Cartimandua, Queen of the Brigantes; he is betrayed to the Romans.	
53	Silures fight on. Ostorius succeeded by unenterprising Didius Gallus.	Marriage of Nero and Octavia, daughter of Claudius.
58	Suetonius Paulinus made Governor; marches into Wales.	St. Paul imprisoned in Rome.
60	Paulinus reaches Menai Straits, invades Anglesey and attacks Druids. Revolt of Boadicea; Colchester sacked; IX Legion cut to pieces; St. Albans and London destroyed. Victory of Suetonius Paulinus; massacre of Britons. Suicide of Boadicea. Reprisals taken: Britons hunted down.	Nero establishing his personal brand of Oriental-type despotism in Rome. Neglects to cultivate the army, notably the Praetorian Guard. St. Paul brought to trial in Rome; appeals and is released.
61	Suetonius Paulinus recalled to Rome; replaced by Turpilianus.	
63-69	Trebellius Maximus Governor. Comparative peace in Britain; Romanization of Britons.	Rome burns in a nine days' fire; Christians blamed and persecuted. Death of Nero; succeeded by Otho then by Vespasian.
71	Brigantes restless. Cerialis sent to subdue them.	New buildings begun in Rome under Vespasian; Nero's buildings destroyed.
74	Julius Frontinus Governor; suppresses Welsh tribes.	Censorship of Vespasian and Titus.

	EVENTS IN BRITAIN	EVENTS IN ROME AND THE EMPIRE
78	Julius Agricola Governor. Extinguishes Welsh and Brigantine resistance.	Tacitus: *Dialogue on Orators*.
79	Agricola advances north along eastern coast from York to the Tweed.	Death of Vespasian. Accession of Titus. Eruption of Vesuvius buries Pompeii.
81	Agricola master of Scotland as far as the Forth and Clyde.	Death of Titus. Accession of Domitian.
83	Agricola thrusts into Highlands. Victory over Caledonians at Mons Graupius.	Domitian crosses Rhine against Chatti; begins building series of defensive forts and ramparts.
84-97	Agricola recalled at climax of Governorship to bring aid to Domitian's campaign on continent. Scanty records exist for this period.	Death of Agricola in Rome, 93 A.D. Assassination of Domitian, 96 A.D. Publication of Tacitus' *Life of Agricola* and *Germania*, c. 97 A.D.
98	Avidius Quietus Governor (until 103 A.D.).	Trajan becomes first provincial Emperor (born near Seville).
117		Hadrian becomes Emperor.
120	Revolt of Brigantes; defeat IX Legion at York.	Death of Tacitus.
122-7	Emperor Hadrian visits Britain. Platorius Nepos constructs Hadrian's Wall from Tyne to Solway Firth.	Hadrian travels extensively in provinces. Has many new buildings erected, particularly in Greece.
140-3	Lollius Urbicus builds the Antonine Wall across Forth-Clyde isthmus.	

	EVENTS IN BRITAIN	EVENTS IN ROME AND THE EMPIRE
180	Caledonian eruption through Antonine Wall. Military initiative passes from Romans to their enemies.	Commodus succeeds Marcus Aurelius as Emperor. Unrest on Rhine and Danube frontiers.
184	Ulpius Marcellus pacifies Britain.	Commodus assumes title "Britannicus" to commemorate victory in Britain.
185	Helvius Pertinax succeeds Ulpius Marcellus. Suppresses mutiny of Roman army in Britain.	
193	Clodius Albinus, successor of Pertinax in Britain, proclaimed Emperor by British legions; crosses with troops to Gaul.	Assassination of Commodus. Pertinax elected Emperor by Praetorian Guard; then murdered by them. Civil war in Rome. Septimius Severus seizes power.
196	All north England overrun by barbarians after removal of garrison by Albinus. Fall of Hadrian's Wall, York, Chester.	Severus marches on Albinus at Lyons. Albinus defeated and killed.
208	Recurrence of trouble in Britain; Severus himself leads campaign. Attacks Caledonians; withdraws to Hadrian's Wall, which he rebuilds.	Severus leaves Rome for Britain.
211	Death of Severus at York. Pacification so effective that Britain enjoys peace, unlike continent, for many years.	Caracalla murders a colleague and a brother on death of Severus to become sole Emperor. Frequent attacks on all frontiers; revolts in some areas.

	EVENTS IN BRITAIN	EVENTS IN ROME AND THE EMPIRE
286	Aurelius Carausius, Roman commander of British fleet, proclaims himself Emperor of an independent Britain.	Diocletian and Maximian acknowledge Carausius as one of the Augusti.
293	Constantius Chlorus instructed to seize Carausius' French possessions. Allectus murders Carausius, replaces him.	Constantius and Galerius appointed Caesars in West and East respectively.
297	Constantius crosses Channel. Defeats Allectus, reorganizes Britain.	Galerius defeats Narses and recovers Mesopotamia.
306	Death of Constantius at York after protracted encounter with Picts.	Constantine the Great, son of Constantius, assumes title of Caesar Imperator.
368	Spanish Count Theodosius clears out barbarians established in Britain.	Reign of Valentinian. Picts, Scots, Saxons, Franks and Attacotti make concerted attacks on the Empire; Roman troops routed.
383	Britain left defenceless; last stand made at Hadrian's Wall. Wholesale barbarian invasions.	Magnus Maximus denudes Britain of its garrison to seize Empire from Gratian, son of Valentinian.
393	Stilicho, regent of Theodosius, liberates Britain.	
396 to 402	Stilicho enlists help of Cunedda (British chieftain) to help pacify Britain.	Stilicho forced to use British troops to drive Visigoths out of Greece. Alaric the Goth defeated at Verona in Italy.

403-6	British troops set up successive usurpers called Marcus, Gratian and Constantine to defend country from invasions.	Fresh Gothic invasion into Italy led by Radagaisus; defeated.
410	Roman legions withdrawn from Britain to protect Rome; effective end of Roman occupation of Britain; Britons left to defend themselves from invasions of Caledonians and German tribes.	Rome captured and sacked by Alaric.

PREHISTORIC BRITAIN UP TO THE ROMANS

Our story begins with the age of Neolithic man
—from 3,000 B.C. onwards. By that time earth-
quakes, volcanic action and glaciers had finished
their work and England's rivers had found
something like their modern level. Inviting
routes lay open for invasions which seem to have
run much the same course many times over.
The invaders, steering in dug-out canoes far
into the country by easy inlets, would then take
the upland drier tracks, conquering the previous
occupants or driving them inland. They would
halt at the Midland forests, or skirt them with
dislike. Finally, they would be arrested by the
rocky hills where the successively displaced cultures
could find refuge, and the new world painfully
and very slowly fuse with the old. From such
fusion—in Wales, Scotland and elsewhere—would
emerge something very different from the pattern
triumphant in the coastal plain.

Until the first century B.C. all invaders pursued
much the same objectives—they wanted room,
dry grazing and good water. Therefore, though
some would stay to fish and fowl by rivers and
estuaries, most would seek at all costs to get
away from the forests they dreaded, from oak
and ash which their weapons could not cut,

and from clays and water-logged soils where their animals would fare badly. The higher hills they found useful for refuge camps and summer pasture, but in general they made for the upper fringes of the lowland plain. Thus relics of their dwelling places, their tombs and ornaments have been found thickest on the Thames gravel terraces, the chalk downs of northern Wessex, the porous water-bearing ridges which stretch from the Severn to east Yorkshire, or the East Anglian heaths. In such regions, connected by trackways of unknown antiquity, and above all in the Salisbury Plain centre, lay the heart of the first historic England.

These early civilizations overlapped, so that clear divisions of time are difficult to determine. Thus flint arrow heads persisted for ages after the introduction of bronze, and barrow burials continued up to the time of the Romans. Moreover any particular migration or culture might affect only one small part of the island: in the hill regions, especially Dartmoor or the Yorkshire moors, life went on with little visible change, or changed in different ways than the oft-conquered south.

The first written account of Britain comes from the Greek Pytheas of Marseilles, who explored its coasts about 325 B.C.; before that we must depend upon what archaeology can make of camps and hut-circles, metal weapons, ornaments and pottery,

193

or on anthropology's deduction from discovered skeletons and later human types, or the verdict of philology regarding speech development. It is often practically impossible to separate evidence of invasion from evidence of trade, or to build conclusions on the grave ornaments of many centuries during which some settlers inhumed their dead and others cremated them.

The little we can detect of Neolithic man is all-important. In the third millennium before Christ, there were three invasions of Britain—a northern one from the Baltic area, one from southern France; and a third dominant stock arrived by way of the Atlantic and the Irish Sea. The majority of these were people of a dark, slight, long-headed Mediterranean type, flintminers who had domesticated animals and sowed a little wheat.

From about 1,900 to 1,000 B.C., there followed what are styled the Early and Middle Bronze Ages, though where and by what divided is less easy to say. The so-called "Beaker Folk" who began this new set of invasions, if originally of Mediterranean stock, absorbed in their wanderings some Nordic strain since broader heads and a sturdier build marked them out from their predecessors. Most appear to have come last from the Rhineland and settled in great numbers over the whole east, from the Yorkshire wold to the Thames estuary. They inhumed their dead in

many sorts of round barroxs and may have practised human sacrifice. Bronze, mixed perhaps from Irish copper and Cornish tin, was the material used by their chieftains and fighting men, and was a medium of their trade, which also embraced a flourishing commerce in Irish gold and jet from Yorkshire. They were a more organized people than any yet existent in Britain, since the first works at Stonehenge and the circles of Avebury date from this era. Theirs was the power that brought giant blue stones from Pembrokeshire to Salisbury Plain, cut ditches fifty feet deep and morticed lintels into vast shaped uprights.

From about 1,000 B.C. we enter the Late Bronze Age which shades, by degrees unproven, into the Early Iron Age around 500 B.C. It is an age primarily of amalgamation of conquerors and conquered, of population expansion by a people who wove cloth and smelted charcoal, introduced a rude plough to carve out the small rectangular terraced fields, still visible on the downs and, most marked of all, greatly increased the quantity and quality of metal-working. New types of metal work were introduced—socketed and hollow-cast axes, swords with a cutting edge, and sickles, wheeled vehicles and cauldrons. Arts and crafts appearing at this time seem to denote new immigrations—of an Alpine element and of a western link with Spain—but although both of these were to recur, it is true to say that from this time on the trend of immigration came predominantly from the North, notably from the Rhineland and the Ardennes. We have, in fact, reached the epoch of the Celts and the beginning of those folk-wanderings which for a thousand years convulsed Europe.

Caesar called the inhabitants of Britain, "Britanni" and the island, "Britannia," evidently confusing the more correct form "Pretanni" which the Greek explorer Pytheas found in Gaul. But by Caesars's time the majority of the inhabitants of Britain were Celtic, like the Gauls. They were part of a powerful nation called variously Keltoi, Celtae, Galatae and Galli by the inhabitants of the Mediterranean basin. Not a unified nation in the modern sense, the Celts were a people composed of tribes of varying size, usually politically independent of one another but with certain common characteristics, which first became apparent in the area north of the Alps at the beginning of the sixth century B.C. It was at this time that the iron-using warrior chieftains, centred on Hallstatt in Austria, first gained power, and from this base they expanded west, east and south—as far east as Asia Minor, where they gave their name to Galatia, and in the west to Spain and Britain. They plundered Greece and Italy, and in 390 B.C. a group of them, returning from a raid in central Italy, captured Rome and held it to ransom.

The Mediterranean peoples recognized in them at once a people different from themselves, taller and more powerfully built, fairer in skin and hair (their blondness accentuated by their custom of washing their hair in lime), blue-eyed and differently dressed, wearing trousers and tunic. They were certainly taller than the average Roman, and more warlike also. The lure of the rich civilizations in Italy was a powerful magnet for a people fond of personal adornment, such as gold torcs. After 390 B.C. nearly two centuries were to pass before the Romans were able to master the Celts settled in northern Italy; and the remainder of the continental Celts, in Gaul, were not defeated until the campaigns of Julius Caesar.

How precisely, and when, the Celtic invaders affected the British Isles is disputed in every detail. Two different families of Celtic tongues were later developed, respectively called Goidel ("Q" Celtic, retaining the original Indo-European "Q" sound) represented by Irish and Gaelic, and Brythonic or Gallo-Brittonic ("P" Celtic, modifying the "Q" sound to "P") represented by Gaulish, with insular versions in Welsh, Cornish and Breton. But it is still not known when that distinction was made, whether before or after reaching these islands. In one way or another archaeology seems to establish a continuous arrival of many groups of Celts from about 800 to 450 B.C., coming from Swiss lake-villages, from Cham-

197

pagne and Brittany, and even more so from the northern French and lower Rhine regions, where Celt and Teuton had met and mixed. They made their way to Scarborough headland, into the Fens and the Thames and the Hampshire harbours; another wave, sailing from the Atlantic ports, reached the tin workings that exported through St. Michael's Mount, and by way of the Severn passed into the Midlands.

These tall, fair-haired people called the natives whom they defeated "Pretanni" or painted folk. They were experienced warriors and brought with them the power of iron—later on they would mine the ores of the Sussex Weald and the Forest of Dean—making six-foot ash-hafted spears, chariots with iron-rimmed wheels, and horse harness. They were the builders of the fortified camps which stud many cape promontories and all the southern downs, often with vast ditches and guarded gates—Maiden Castle in Dorset is a famous example. Their pottery and carefully-wrought brooches and artistic bronze work suggest a wide trade and a powerful aristocracy. Between 250 B.C. and about 100 A.D. we have evidence of two further, widely separated settlements, well advanced in culture. One, identified in Yorkshire, which spread through the Fens to East Anglia, is of a people who buried their chieftains with horse and chariot and daggers; while far away at Glastonbury other invaders raised log-platform dwellings over the marshes and worked in iron, bronze, stone and bone, also smelting lead and killing man or game with pellets from slings.

About 75 B.C. began a final sequence of Celtic invasions which were to bind Britain in a permanent relation with Europe. Some twenty-one years before Caesar the third and most advanced group of all, the Belgae, who would prove his most powerful enemies, began to arrive in Britain. Centred on the Marne and Aisne, and part-German in culture, they had already won some footing in these areas when they appeared in force in Kent, headed by the trite of the Catuvellauni, and spread from thence over the Thames basin into Essex and Hertfordshire, where at Wheathampstead they began building a fortified capital, while lesser branches continued on to the Midland streams lying between Oxford and Cambridge. The enormous earthwork at Wheathampstead was the headquarters of Cassivellaunus, leader of the Catuvellauni, who was responsible for the chief opposition to Caesar—it was successfully stormed during Caesar's second campaign. Formal tribute was then exacted and further expansion forbidden, but before long the Catuvellauni had transferred their mint and presumably their tribal centre from Hertfordshire to Camulodunum (Colchester), conquering the Trinovantes of Essex.

Some thirty years after the first Belgic invasion, when Caesar had come and gone, another Belgic tribe, the Atrebates, refugees from Roman power, crossed from Normandy, fixed a capital at Silchester in Berkshire, and ruthlessly attacked the peoples of West Sussex and Somerset. The Belgae brought with them a rude vigour, and some positive improvements such as the introduction of a heavier form of plough which could really turn the sod, and they undertook a certain amount of land clearance. From the horse of their chariots perhaps descends the white horse cut on the Berkshire downs.

Although their power was considerable enough to make sizeable states, at the opening of the Christian era we find many British kingdoms, and no united Britain or a uniform culture. Outside the two substantial Belgic states mentioned, there survived strong Celtic communities; the Dobuni, extending from the Cotswolds to the Welsh foothills, with one wing stretched into Dorset; the Trinovantes in Essex, the Iceni in East Anglia, and the Brigantes in the north. Both in the north and in the Cornish west and Wales, a bronze age civilization, or an even ruder life, was perpetuated, ranging from chiefs in hill-forts down to villages of pit-dwellings or stone huts. The Belgic areas were wealthy, with much wheat-growing and iron-making, but a finer sense of art lived on in the Celtic middle west, where pottery retained the bold curves and spirals of an earlier age, and from which some magnificent bronze ornament was derived. Everywhere we seem to stumble on separate communities, sometimes wholly disconnected, sometimes at war with one another. Whether Breton immigrants defending Maiden Castle with slings, subterranean dwellers in Wales, pile-dwellers in Yorkshire or merely isolated farmers, all alike were barely touched by the series of conquests.

The coinage of the different British chiefs or kings reflected their different policies, and illustrated also the growth of trade and social complexity in pre-Roman Britain. By 100 B.C. a gold coinage had emerged in many areas, replaced later by silver and bronze, which in turn had gradually replaced the currency of iron bars or ingots attested by Caesar and apparently of the form of sword blanks of standard weight. The coinage of the Atrebates closely copies Roman originals and bears the Latin word "rex," a sign that the Atrebates knew some Latin, for the word was anathema to the Romans but was granted to allies of the Roman people. One coin issued by the Catuvellauni, by contrast, bears the Celtic word "ricon," meaning king like "rex," but by its choice of language probably indicating independence of Rome. Likewise the Catuvellaunian coinage was designed in spirited artistic independence of the Roman coinage. One difference between the two British coinages is particularly striking: that of Cunobelinus, leader of the Catuvellauni (Shakespeare's Cymbeline), carries an ear of barley while that of Commius of the Atrebates shows a vine leaf, extolling the merits of wine imported from the Roman world rather than British beer!

In art these tribes possessed a native late-Celtic style, descended from far-off Mediterranean antecedents and more directly connected with the La Tène culture of the continental Celts. Its characteristics were a flamboyant and fantastic treatment of plant, animal and, more rarely, human forms, a brilliant use of curved, geometrical forms and much skill in enamelling. Its finest products were achieved in bronze, but the same patterns spread to woodwork and pottery.

For a generation before 43 A.D. the Belgae had thrown open their territories to Roman commercial enterprise. Some decades before the establishment of Roman rule, Roman or Romanized craftsmen were working in the service of Belgic kings such as Tasciovanus and Cunobelinus. Roman bronzes, Roman pottery, Roman silver vessels were trafficked in Britain in return for (as Strabo tells us) corn, cattle, gold, silver, iron, skins, slaves and hunting dogs. An astonishing result of the excavation of Cymbeline's capital at Colchester was the discovery of some of the finest products of Italian factories on the floors of the primitive hutments of the Belgic population. The

Roman invader, following the Roman trafficker, was confronted with this curious and paradoxical mixture of commercial prosperity and native squalor.

It can be seen that the political system of the Celts was essentially tribal and in fact non-political. Their traditions and temperament were those of an incurably nomadic people, as volatile and lightfooted as the half-wild herds driven and corralled by their forefathers. In both Britons and Gauls Tacitus notes the same audacity in provoking danger, and irresolution in facing up to it. The frequent absence of a permanent water supply in their hill towns is characteristic of them in their proto-historical environment; on the cut-and-run principle of warfare, provision for a momentary siege was adequate. Wars were waged between meals.

Similarly their essays in political development appear to have been lacking in certainty and direction. Occasionally a tribal king would acquire by force or diplomacy a suzerainty over neighbouring tribes, normally a transient union. On the other hand, there was a tendency in Caesar's time for the tribal councils to increase their authority at the expense of the kinglet, and sometimes an oligarchical system of government succeeded, at least momentarily, the monarchical. The Celtic world was ill at ease in its new environment,

203

riddled with faction and irresolution; its conquest by Rome was not premature. Celtic Europe was thereby enabled to pass through the discipline of Roman paganism, and thereafter to reassert itself for a while in the gentler precincts of the Romano-Celtic church.

BRITAIN AS A ROMAN PROVINCE

Had Caesar never lived, the destiny of Rome must have taken her to the Atlantic. She had destroyed Carthage, absorbed Greece, crushed Asia Minor and carried her frontier to the Euphrates. Only on the north and northwest was she exposed to the barbarians who, since the first Celtic drive three centuries before, had never rested. To meet the emergency they had created in Gaul, Caesar accepted a five-years' command in 58 B.C. In three successful campaigns he removed the threat and at midsummer in 55 B.C. decided on an exploratory expedition to Britain as a preliminary to conquest.

After the departure of Julius Caesar from Britain the Island was not troubled by Rome for nearly ninety years. In that interval Caesar destroyed Pompey and was himself slain, Mark Antony and Octavian fought over the succession, Tiberius reigned, and Christ was crucified, while the British scene saw the important transfer of power from the Trinovantes to the Catuvellauni, whose chief began to style himself "King of the Britons." All this while Roman sentiment expected, and even demanded, the annexation of Britain.

The Empire established by Augustus gave the Mediterranean world for the first time a single political form. There was one Emperor over all, one army, one civil service and in the end one religion, although it was never possible to speak of one nationality or one culture. During his forty-five years of unchallenged power, ending with his death in 14 A.D., Augustus consolidated the far-flung provinces, established a large degree of local self-government in them, revitalized the economy, stabilized the Treasury, created a widespread and heretofore unmatched prosperity, reduced, disciplined and tamed the Army, arranged for his successor (while signally failing to establish an acceptable system for later selections) and, in the process of all this achievement, introduced to history the comparative felicity of the Pax Romana—order, peace and obedience to law within the long-battered world of Mediterranean civilisation. His success, so monumental in character, so lasting in history, rested on his understanding and practical use of two Roman creations long antecedent to his reign, both of which he developed and moulded to serve his farsighted purpose: the Law and the Army.

When Augustus planned the stabilisation of the Empire he seems originally to have intended to make its northern boundary in Europe the River Elbe. Through the lands between that river and the Rhine, his generals, Drusus and later Tiberius, brought about the sullen submission of the surly forest tribes. With this pacification apparently complete, Tiberius turned over his command to

Quintilius Varus, who in 9 A.D. allowed his army of three legions to be ambushed and totally destroyed in the trackless wastes of the Teutoburg Forest. Augustus, appalled, summarily gave up hopes of further expansion and set the Rhine and the Danube on the north and the Channel on the west as the Imperial frontiers, earnestly recommending to his successors that they go no farther afield.

Nevertheless his awareness of popular opinion in Rome made Augustus careful to convey, through his court poets, the impression that the conquest of Britain was always imminent. Tiberius followed this example, for it seems that although the island of Britain lay on the fringes of Roman influence and came late within the sphere of Rome, the imaginations of all classes of the Roman people were stirred by the idea of annexing Britain.

Thus Tiberius, like Augustus, may have contemplated invasion but never initiated it. The reasons are not hard to find: his policy was one of consolidation rather than of expansion; moreover the Augustan settlement, the "Principate," held within itself a contradiction which made it difficult for the machinery of Imperial government to embark upon a policy of foreign conquest. The system inaugurated by Augustus demanded that the Emperor preside over a delicately-balanced administration in which one party (the Princeps) held the reality of power and another party (the Senate) held the semblance of it. This system was not of Tiberius' making and probably not to his liking, yet he had to direct its further development. To this fault in the constitution created by Augustus can in fact be traced the fundamental weakness which brought increasing instability into Roman political life and made it a prey to the corrupt intrigues of various factions surrounding the Imperator—a weakness which spread through the hierarchy of soldiers and civil servants serving the far-flung empire and in time brought it to its knees.

During the reign of these first two emperors, the internal condition of the Empire steadily improved. The Gallic provinces in particular, reaching to the Rhine, speedily embraced the standards of Roman civilisation, and participated fully in its economic life. Tranquillity and order, peaceful trade and commerce, replaced the quarelling anarchy the Gallic peoples had known before Caesar. In three generations, with only occasional flare-ups, the concept of being part of a civilised world community had taken root and flourished. The resulting prosperity was not without effect across the Channel in Britain, where raiding one's neighbour was a traditional and honoured means of livelihood. This had indeed been so in Gaul before Caesar; but in Britain it remained a way of life, subject to possible retribution, but never to moral condemnation.

The irritations and the compensating satisfactions of a growing commerce with Britain were another factor in the increasing interest with which Roman officials looked across the Channel, and an added incentive was provided by the fury of the Druid priesthood. Refugees from Gaul, opposing the imposition of Roman customs and law, fled to Britain and there harangued their faithful followers on the crimes of Roman tyranny. As Gaul became Roman in thought, language and custom Britain, in the eyes of many peaceful provincials, as well as in those of the responsible officials, was slowly becoming a nuisance. Whereas Augustus considered the Channel a frontier that required no defence, the Britons, in their greed for other people's property and their capacity for intrigue, proved it otherwise.

Gaius Caesar, "Caligula," succeeded his great-uncle without incident on March 18th, 37 A.D. More truly a Julian than his father Germanicus, he conceived that a revival of the scheme to conquer Britain would enable him to get to know the army, and would fire the popular imagination. The pretext was at hand—that a renegate British prince, Adminius (Amminius) son of Cunobelinus, had submitted to him personally and requested his aid. According to the historian, Suetonius, who

loved gossip more than history, Caligula interpreted
the personal submission and request for aid of
Adminius as carrying with it the submission of the
entire island. Be this as it may, he abruptly ceased
his "pseudo-military clowning" on the Rhine in
the spring of 40 and marched what troops were
on hand to the Channel, in the meantime ordering
ships to be made ready.

It is virtually impossible to assess whether
Caligula intended this conquest or merely imagined
it. It seems probable that his troops behaved at
this stage as those of Claudius two years later
and refused to embark, and that Caligula could
not wait for them to recover their nerve for fear
of what might be happening back in Italy. The
most he could do was to issue a public manifesto
formally announcing the annexation of Britain.
The actual military occupation he could not
attempt and perhaps was incapable of. He returned to Italy in August with his mind a prey to the
suspicions and fears which the conspiracy of his
nearest relatives had engendered. In 41 he died
in Rome, killed by a tribune of the Praetorian
Guard. His short reign brought into startling
relief the despotism inherent in the Principate
and the hopeless dependence of the Senate on the
Emperor.

Contemplating their deed, the murderers must
have realised that their sole hope of safety lay in
selecting the next incumbent. Chancing on a

grandson of Augustus, Tiberius Claudius Drusus Germanicus, they convinced him that his duty to Rome required not only his ascent to the Principate but the payment to them of a liberal donative for supporting his candidacy. Claudius agreed—it is difficult to see how he could have refused, and have lived. He further agreed to the suggestion of a new conquest, to be followed by a glittering triumph and the honorific title "Britannicus," bestowed by vote of the Senate. In fact, given the spirit of the times, the arguments for the conquest of Britain had by now become nearly unanswerable.

Claudius had a keen sense of Rome's historical mission, believing that Rome should assimilate, as well as expand by setting up client kingdoms: he coveted the title of "Extender of Empire." In invading Britain he could plead that he was fulfilling a civilising mission to stamp out barbaric rites, was ensuring the integrity of Gaul, and was safeguarding Roman traders and exploiting British wealth in the form of metal, timber, cattle and slaves. However his chief motive was undoubtably the conviction that Roman public opinion strongly favoured the adventure.

From the time of Caesar onwards the opportunity Britain afforded for the winning of prestige and military honour, and the satisfying of personal ambition, provided the principal motive for Roman

212

interference. Caesar himself probably hoped to refill his war chest from the much-rumoured British wealth, as well as from the sale of prisoners; the Claudian invaders, too, came expecting to find considerable mineral wealth. They were disappointed in this, but they did find in Britain a lowland area which could be easily controlled, but with too much woodland for intensive cultivation, and a highland area which they were to hold loosely and never properly exploit. The best tribute that Britain would bring to Rome was her man-power for the Imperial armies; the invaders soon realised that the economic and financial liabilities would outweigh any gains that might be won. Strabo stated his opinion quite clearly: Britain should *not* be conquered, because the profits to be derived therefrom would not even cover the cost of the garrisons which would have to be maintained there.

Thus after the Claudian conquest Britain lost the El Dorado character it had previously held for imaginative Romans and even became, as the remotest of all the provinces, something of a Roman Siberia for troublemakers, both political and religious—it is recorded of Marcus Aurelius that in the 170's, when he had to deal with Tiridates, a dissident native ruler in the East, "Marcus did not put him to death, but merely sent him to Britain." But for its first 150 years as a province Britain was one of the senior appointments for a Senator with military ambitions; a theatre in which renown could be won to justify the celebration of a triumph at home. Moreover the addition of the legions stationed on the island of Britain and the fleet at the disposal of the Governor altered the delicate balance of military power among the various frontier commanders.

This was a danger that Augustus had been well aware of—he had found from personal experience that loyalty to a general rather than to Rome was the major motivation of the legions—and had laid down a policy that the forces entrusted to the several provincial governors, while necessarily varying in size according to their military responsibilities, should in no single case be large enough to make a particular governor, on the death of an emperor, a nearly unchallengeable candidate for the succession. But nothing was ever set up to ensure the maintenance of this policy—nor could it have been, as every succeeding emperor became increasingly dependent on military power. Any sucessful general became a source of anxiety to the Emperor. Thus Suetonius, for his success in suppressing Boadicea's rebellion, suffered the fate reserved for Nero's abler commander: he was recalled to Rome, unhonoured, in 61 A.D. Britain became the ideal province in which a Governor might consolidate his power and build up his forces undisturbed, prior to making a bid for the Empire itself, as the careers

of Clodius Albinus (193-196) and of Magnus Maximus (c. 383) clearly illustrate.

The vitality of Roman Britain and the grasp which Roman administration had over the province of Britain is well symbolised by the fortunes of Hadrian's Wall. Built between the years 121 and 127 A.D. by the Emperor Hadrian's friend and governor of Britain, Nepos, its construction reflected Agricola's pacification of the country and the conviction, which always followed the first flush of conquest, that Rome would last forever. Falling in 196 to the Caledonians, it was almost immediately rebuilt by Governor Senecio; not until 383 was it breached by the northern hordes for the last time, as a result of the removal of British garrisons by Magnus Maximus in his bid for the imperial throne. Then wholesale barbarian invasions of Roman Britain followed, but these did not or could not entirely destroy the wall—it stands today as perhaps the most tangible memorial to Roman power in Britain.

The Roman occupation of Britain lasted for as long as 360 years, and to divide this time into a period of offensive conquest and one of defensive peace seems to blur the main truth. For if within forty years of the Claudian conquest Roman armies reached the extremities of Wales and Scotland, several times a military disaster or rebellion threatened a premature end to the entire

Roman occupation. The story seems rather one of a border province, always weakly held, and often with inferior troops, responding instantly to a spell of good government in Rome, but in its own character never self-sufficient, and drawing all its energy from the heart of the Empire. When Rome sagged under Nero, or rose in new glory under the Antonines in the second century, was restored in the fourth by Constantine, and broke at last before the Goths and Huns, so, correspondingly, Roman power in Britain faltered, flowed again and then ran dry. There were years of a forward policy and years of economy, but the disease of Empire was incurable. A date can be found after which the loss of Britain was certain, although the end is best visualised not as one of sudden, fierce destruction, but rather as a fading away into a slow, long-drawn-out dusk.

BRITAIN AS SEEN BY THE ROMAN HISTORIANS

The most rewarding classical descriptions of the Celts are those by Diodorus Siculus and Strabo, who wrote at or shortly after the time of the Roman conquest of Gaul and were therefore in a position to describe the Gauls of France in their pre-Roman state. The Celts of Britain must have been very similar.

In stature [declare Diodorus] they are tall, with rippling muscles and white skins: red-haired, not only naturally but they do all they can to make it redder by art. They often wash their hair in water boiled with lime, and turn it backward from the forehead to the crown of the head, and thence to their very necks, that their faces may be more fully seen, so that they look like satyrs and hobgoblins... The persons of quality shave their chins close, but their moustaches they let fall so low that they even cover their mouths: when they eat their meat hangs dangling by their hair, and when they drink the liquor runs through their moustaches as through a sieve... In the very midst of feasting, upon any small occasion it is ordinary for them to rise, and, without any regard for their lives, to fall to with their swords... In their journeys and fights they use chariots drawn with two horses, which carry a charioteer and a soldier, and when they meet horsemen in the battle they fall upon their enemies with their throwing-spears then, quitting their chariots, they set to with their swords... When at any time they cut off their enemies' heads they hang them about their horses' necks.

Their clothing seemed strange to Graeco-Roman eyes. Unlike the more barbaric Germans, whom Tacitus describes as "either naked or lightly covered with a small mantle," they wore parti-coloured coats with sleeves "interwoven here and there with divers coloured flowers," and wide and flowing trousers (*bracae* or *anaxyrides*)—a costume of oriental origin derived possibly through the Scythians of southern Russia. It may have been introduced thence into the West first by Germans rather than by Celts. The trousered costume was essentially that of a horse-riding people, and it is suggestive that in Caesar's time, when the Germans were thrusting strongly westwards, the old Celtic usage of chariots was, in Gaul, being superseded by cavalry, although in remoter Britain, where breeds of horse large enough for riding were seemingly not yet available, Caesar found the Celtic pony-drawn chariots still in full vogue.

The defensive arms of the Gauls, according to Strabo, were:

> ...a shield proportioned to the height of the man, garnished with their own ensigns... Upon their heads they wore helmets of brass, with large pieces of work raised upon them for ostentation's sake... horns of the same metal or shapes of birds and beasts carved on them. They have trumpets after the barbarian manner, which in sounding make a horrid noise, to strike terror fit and proper for the occasion.
> These people are of a most terrible aspect, and have a most dreadful and loud voice. In their converse they are sparing of words, and speak many things darkly and figuratively... Among them they have poets, who sing melodious songs, whom they call bards, who to their musical instruments, like unto harps, chant forth the praises of some and the dispraises of others... There are likewise among them philosophers or divines whom they call Druids, who are held in veneration and esteem.

In his account of his first invasion of Britain Caesar, writing as usual in the third person, describes how the Roman troops were thrown into confusion "by the novel character of the fighting," so that only his own arrival saved the day: "Caesar brought assistance in the very nick of time, for his coming caused the enemy to halt, and enabled our men to recover from their fear."

After his second invasion he wrote the following account of the inhabitants of Kent:

> Of all the Britons the inhabitants of Kent, an entirely maritime district, are by far the most civilised, differing but little from the Gallic manner of life. Of the inlanders most do not sow corn, but live on milk and flesh and clothe themselves in skins. All the Britons, indeed, dye themselves with woad, which produces a blue colour, and makes their appearance in battle more terrible. They wear long hair, and shave every part of the body save the head and the upper lip. Groups of ten or twelve men have wives together in common, and particularly brothers along with brothers, and fathers with sons; but the children born of the unions are reckoned to belong to the particular house to which the maiden was first conducted.

When evaluating Caesar's accounts it must be understood that, whereas Strabo and Diodorus were concerned with the writing of history and geography, Caesar was an astute politician and military commander writing self-justificatory despatches after the event. Tierney has gone so far as to say that "Caesar had no interest in Gallic ethnography as such," and that the ethnographical

passages in the *Gallic Wars* are there because
literary convention ruled that historical works
should contain such material. Caesar's general,
Hirtius, who wrote the concluding Book VIII of
the work, seems to have been well aware of this.
"Caesar not only wrote with supreme fluency and
elegance," he said, "he also knew superlatively
well how to describe his plans and policies."
Dr. Grant writes moreover that "Caesar's apparent
simplicity and lack of rhetoric were deliberate
artifices based on mastery of the most elaborate
rhetorical theory."

Nevertheless the popular appeal of the *Gallic
Wars* is undeniable and it seems that criticism of
the work is based on the bias with which the
facts are presented to the reader rather than on
inaccurate reporting of them. Here, for instance,
is Caesar's account of his first landing in Britain:

These arrangements made, he caught a spell
of fair weather for sailing, and weighed anchor
about the third watch: he ordered the cavalry
to proceed to the further harbour, embark, and
follow him... He himself reached Britain
about the fourth hour of the day, and there
beheld the armed forces of the enemy displayed
on all the cliffs [near Dover]. Such was the
nature of the ground, so steep the heights
which banked the sea, that a missile could be
hurled from the higher levels on to the shore.

Thinking this place to be by no means suitable
for disembarkation, he waited at anchor till the
ninth hour for the rest of the flotilla to assemble
there... and catching at one and the same
moment a favourable wind and tide, he gave the
signal, and weighed anchor, and moving on
about seven miles from that spot, he grounded
his ships where the shore was even and open
[probably between Walmer and Deal]... Disembarkation was a matter of extreme difficulty
for the following reasons. The ships, on
account of their size, could not be run ashore,
except in deep water; the troops—though they
did not know the ground, had not their hands
free, and were loaded with the grievous weight
of their arms—had nevertheless at one and the
same time to leap down from the vessels, to
stand firm in the waves, and to fight the enemy.
The enemy, on the other hand, had all their
limbs free, and knew the ground exceeding
well; and either standing on dry land or advancing a little way into the water, they boldly
hurled their missiles, or spurred on their horses,
which were trained to it...

While our troops hung back, chiefly on
account of the depth of the sea, the eaglebearer
of the Tenth Legion after a prayer to heaven
to bless the legion by his act, cried: "Leap
down, soldiers, unless you wish to betray your
eagle to the enemy; is shall be told that I at

least did my duty to my country and my general."
When he had shouted this aloud, he cast himself
forth from the ship, and began to bear the eagle
towards the enemy. Then our troops exhorted
one another not to allow so dire a disgrace,
and leapt down from the ship with one accord.
And when the troops on the nearest ships saw
them, they likewise followed on and drew near
to the enemy.

Further difficulties lay in store for navigators
accustomed to the tideless Mediterranean:

That same night, as it chanced, the moon was
full, the day of the month which usually makes
the highest tides in the Ocean, a fact unknown
to our men. Therefore the tide was found to
have filled the warships, in which Caesar had
caused his army to be conveyed across, and which
he had drawn up on dry land; and at the same
time the storm was buffeting the transports,
which were made fast to anchors. Nor had our
troops any chance of handling them or helping.
Several ships went to pieces; and the others,
by loss of cordage, anchors and the rest of their
tackle, were rendered useless for sailing. This
inevitably caused dismay throughout the army.
For there were no other ships to carry them
back; everything needful for the repair of the
ships was lacking; and as it was generally

understood that the army was to winter in Gaul, no corn had been provided in these parts against the winter.

When they became aware of this, the British chiefs who had assembled at Caesar's head-quarters after the fight took counsel together. As they knew that the Romans lacked cavalry, ships, and corn and perceived the scantiness of the army from the smallness of the camp (further emphasized by the fact that Caesar had brought the legions over without baggage), they thought it best to renew the war... for they were confident that when the present force was overcome or cut off from return no one thereafter would cross over to Britain to make war upon them...

If the Britons did count on this, the following year proved how wrong they were; when the Roman fleet hove in sight of land not an enemy was to be seen, "for," says Caesar, "alarmed at the number of ships, 800 of which had been seen at once, they had concealed themselves on high ground away from the shore."

In Book V we are given an account of the campaign against Cassivellaunus—

...whose territories are divided from the maritime states by the river called Thames, about eighty miles from the sea. Hitherto there had been continuous wars between this chief and the other states; but our arrival moved the

Britons to appoint him commander-in-chief for the conduct of the whole campaign...

Having obtained knowledge of their plans, Caesar led his army into the borders of Cassivellaunus as far as the river Thames, which can be crossed at one place only on foot, and that with difficulty. When he had arrived there he noticed that on the other bank of the river a large force of the enemy was drawn up. The bank was fortified with a fringe of sharp projecting stakes, and stakes of the same kind fixed under water were concealed by the stream. When he had learnt these details from prisoners and deserters, Caesar sent the cavalry in advance and ordered the legions to follow up instantly. But the troops moved with such speed and such spirit, although they had only their heads above water, that the enemy could not withstand the assault of legions and cavalry, but abandoned the banks and betook themselves to flight.

When Cassivellaunus had thus relinquished all hope of a struggle, and disbanded the greater part of his force, he kept our marches under observation with the remainder—about 4,000 chariots. Withdrawing a little from the route, he concealed himself in entangled positions among the woods. In whatever districts he had learnt that we intended to march he drove all cattle and human beings from the fields into the woods; then, whenever our cavalry dashed out over the fields to plunder and devastate more freely, he sent out charioteers from the woods by every road and path, engaging our cavalry to their great danger, and preventing them from ranging further afield by the fear thus caused. The only course left to Caesar was to allow no party to remove very far from the main column of the legions, and to do as much harm to the enemy in laying waste the fields and setting fire to the country as the marching powers of the legionaries could accomplish...

The *Life of Agricola* by Tacitus was published with his *Germania* in 97-98 A.D. In the *Agricola* we have a portrait of Britain at the time of Boadicea's revolt written in a style that never loiters, often sparkles, is never dull. The book has exercised a steady attraction on generation after generation for in it can be traced an ideal that commands admiration—belief in Rome, in Roman destiny, and in Roman ways and standards of life. Of the private life of Tacitus we know very little indeed— he married the daughter of Agricola in 77 A.D. but he never mentions her. We know that he was planning to write a general history of the years 68-96 A.D., and the account of Britain might be regarded as a preparative study; but in it the biographical interest is always to the fore—details of both geography and history are cut down to a minimum. Tacitus had the obvious advantage of a close relationship with Agricola, who as a Governor of Britain knew it as no Roman had ever known it before.

Nevertheless it is hard to accept his claim that he put research on a new basis, with solid fact to replace guesswork. He might possibly have done so had he taken more trouble. But he is often amazingly careless about military and geo-graphical detail, and throws the achievements of Agricola on so uncertain a background that they begin to become blurred themselves. He writes as though any province, any provincials, any army, any enemy might serve equally well to illustrate his hero's virtues, as in the following account of events following one of Agricola's victories:

Night brought our men the satisfactions of victory and booty. The Britons wandered all over the countryside, men and women together wailing, carrying off their wounded and calling out to the survivors. They would leave their homes and in fury set fire to them, and choose lairs, only to abandon them at once. Sometimes they would try to concert plans, then break off conference. Sometimes the sight of their dear ones broke their hearts, more often it goaded them to fury. Some, it was afterwards found, laid violent hands on their wives and children in a kind of pity. The next day revealed the quality of the victory more distinctly. A grim silence reigned on every hands, the hills were deserted, only here and there was smoke seen rising from chimneys in the distance, and our scouts found no one to encounter them. When they had been sent out in all directions and had made sure that everything pointed to indiscriminate flight and that the enemy were not massing at any point, Agricola led his army into the territory of the Boresti. Summer was almost over, and it was impossible for operations to be extended over a wider area. There Agricola took hostages and ordered his admiral to coast round Britain. The forces allotted were sufficient, and the terror of Rome had gone before him. Agricola himself, marching slowly in order to inspire terror in fresh nations by his very lack of hurry, placed his infantry and cavalry in winter-quarters.

One of the highlights of Tacitus' account of the career of Agricola in Britain is his description of Boadicea's revolt and the events leading up to it:

The Britons submit to the levy, the tribute and the other charges of Empire with cheerful readiness, provided that there is no abuse.

That they bitterly resent, for they are broken in to obedience, not to slavery...

After the governor Didius Gallus, Suetonius Paulinus enjoyed two years of success, conquering tribes and establishing strong forts. Emboldened thereby to attack the island of Anglesey, which was feeding the native resistance, he exposed himself to a stab in the back.

For the Britons, freed from their repressions by the absences of the dreaded legate, began to discuss the woes of slavery, to compare their wrongs and sharpen their sting in the telling. "We gain nothing by submission except heavier burdens for willing shoulders. Once each tribe had one king, now two are clamped on us—the legate to wreak his fury on our lives, the procurator on our property. We subjects are damned in either case, whether our masters quarrel or agree. Their gangs of centurions or slaves, as the case may be, mingle violence and insult. Nothing is any longer safe from their greed and lust. In war it is the braver who takes the spoil; as things stand with us, it is mostly cowards and shirkers that rob our homes, kidnap our children and conscript our men. Any cause is good enough for us to die for—any but our country's. But what a mere handful our invaders are, if we reckon up our own numbers. The Germans, reckoning so, threw off the yoke, and they had only a river, not the Ocean, to shield them. We have country, wives and parents to fight for; the Romans have nothing but greed and self-indulgence. Back they will go, as the deified Julius went back, if only we can rival the valour of our fathers. We must not be scared by the loss of one battle or even two; success may foster the spirit of offense, but it is suffering that gives the power to endure. The gods themselves are at last showing mercy to us Britons in keeping the Roman general away, with his army exiled in another island. For ourselves we have already taken the most difficult step—we have begun to plot. And in an enterprise like this there is more danger in being caught plotting than in taking the plunge.

Goaded by such mutual encouragements, the whole island rose under the leadership of Boadicea, a lady of royal descent—for Britons make no distinction of sex in their leaders. They hunted down the Roman troops in their scattered posts, stormed the forts and assaulted the colony itself, in which they saw their slavery focused; nor did the angry victors deny themselves any form of savage cruelty. In fact, had not Paulinus, on hearing of the revolt, made speed to help, Britain would have been lost. As it was, he restored it to its old obedience by a single successful action. But many guilty rebels refused to lay down their arms out of a peculiar dread of the legate. Fine officer though he was, he seemed likely to abuse their unconditional surrender and punish with undue severity wrongs which he insisted on making personal. The government therefore replaced him by Petronius Turpilianus. They hoped that he would be more merciful and readier to forgive offences to which he was a stranger. He composed the existing troubles, but risked no further move before handing over his province to Trebellius Maximus. Trebellius was deficient in energy and without military experience, but he governed his province like a gentleman. The barbarians now learned, like any Romans, to condone seductive vices, while the intervention of our Civil Wars gave a reasonable excuse for inactivity. There was, however, a serious outbreak of mutiny, for the troops, accustomed to campaigns, ran riot in peace. Trebellius fled and hid to escape his angry army. His self-respect and dignity compromised, he now commanded merely on sufferance. By a kind of tacit bargain the troops kept their licence, the general his life, and the mutiny stopped short of bloodshed. Vettius Bolanus, likewise, as the Civil War still ran its course, declined to disturb Britain by enforcing discipline. There still the same paralysis in face of the foe, the same indiscipline in the camp—only Bolanus was a decent man, with no sins to make him hated, and had won affection where he lacked authority.

But when Vespasian in the course of his general triumph, recovered Britain, there came a succession of great generals and splendid armies, and the hopes of our enemies dwindled.

33. A rude statue of a forest god from Gaul embodies all the mystery and horror of the Druid cult, with its tree worship and human sacrifice. Druidism was widespread amongst the Celts, from Gaul to the British Isles.

THE DRUIDS

The gods of the Britons were many and of all sorts—gods of war and thunder, or local deities of some holy well or haunted wood. The Scottish forests were especially feared as the dwelling place of demons. But the chief feature of their religion was the priesthood of the Druids which, as in Gaul, practised magical arts and horrific rites of human sacrifice, taught a secret lore, and wielded great influence in society. The Britons like the Gauls deferred to the Druid caste, with whom lay the secrets of their sacred songs, the taking of auspices, the award of punishment and the dread power of "taboo," which created a class of untouchables. Unfortunately there exists no written or archaeological evidence to tell us of the spiritual life in Britain. The centre at Glastonbury and the forts outside Winchester and Chichester fell to the Belgae before new towns were built on the ancient sites, first by the Belgic tribes themselves, later by the Romans, thus confusing and obscuring the archaeological evidence.

Moreover the Celtic world, like the rest of barbarian Europe, held to the non-literate oral tradition, which was of course the time-honoured and socially approved method for the conservation and transmission of law, genealogy, story, song and myth in the vernacular. The Druids were in fact specifically charged with the preservation and continuance of this ancient tradition, which deliberately avoided the use of writing. No authentic pre-Christian inscription includes any word for "Druid" in Greek, Latin or Celtic forms, and all the written evidence for Celtic religion belongs to the latest phase, when Gaul and Britain had been incorporated in the Roman Empire. Our earliest tolerably reliable evidence about Druids comes from Julius Caesar and his sources —especially the Stoic philosopher Posidonius, whose work is no longer extant; but three later Greek authors, the historian Diodorus Siculus, the geographer Strabo, and the writer of miscellanies, Athenaeus, have reproduced parts of his writings. The material on the Druids in Caesar's *Gallic Wars* is taken from Posidonius, without acknowledgement and with significant additions, and exaggerations.

For the following two generations little is heard of the Druids—tradition merely states that they were banned by Tiberius and Claudius on account of superstitions and human sacrifices, while Pliny in his *Natural History* enlarges on the magical cures possessed by "this race of prophets and physicians." No classical writer ever fully described or even uncovered the philosophy of the Druids, which was elusive and exerted no influence on classical thought. The understanding of the barbarian world around them by the classical *literati* was inevitably coloured by contemporary modes of thought and current philosophical schemes. Thus Posidonius wrote from the Stoic viewpoint, stylizing the Druids as representative of the *logos* or higher power of the soul.

When we come to the Renaissance rediscovery of the past, and the incidental rediscovery of the Druids, we find them recreated by men who were themselves steeped in the philosophy and scholarship of the Greek and Roman thinkers who had first commented upon this obscure barbarian priesthood. The climate of thought was congenial to an acceptance and a development of the classical philosophers' view, and when fashion shifted from classical to romantic, the Druids were quietly waiting to take on a new life in the contemporary modes of Western thought and emotion. And so, as curiously satisfactory symbols, they have kept their place for a couple of thousand years or more: barbarian sages, primeval Christians, champions of liberty, repositories of mysterious wisdom. Certainly the tradition about them stands in need of reappraisal in the light of modern scholarship and archaeology.

The word DRUI (neuter plural DRUID) is found in Old Irish and may be analysed as DRU-UID or DRU-VID, the second element of which means "he who knows" or "the far-seeing," and the first element of which may be either an intensive prefix or the word meaning "oak."

How far in fact the Druids were originally a Celtic or even Aryan institution is itself a moot point. It is sometimes argued that when the Celts appeared in history Druidism was already in decline and the military caste of Aryan Celts were in revolt against this foreign priesthood, which had previously conquered them. Caesar observes that "their sacred lore is believed to have originated in Britain and to have been carried thence to Gaul; and today those who wish to study it deeply, as a rule cross to Britain to learn it." The relative antiquity which this prestige implies for the Druidic organization in Britain, on the fringe of the Celtic world, does indeed suggest a non-Celtic origin for the system. About 500 B.C., according to Caesar, Druidism spread from Britain to Gaul. Megalithic monuments have been taken as evidence that Druidism flourished in neolithic Ireland and spread thence to Britain well before 500 B.C., finding its refuge in Ireland again after the Roman conquest. But if this is so, and Druidism is of pre-Celtic origin, it is at least evident that the cult and priesthood had become thoroughly naturalized in the Celtic world by the first century B.C. After that time the Druids were members of an Indo-European social order, practising a religion which probably contained many elements by then already ancient.

Druids were encountered in person, probably by Posidonius, certainly by Caesar; Suetonius

Paulinus and his army were publicly cursed by Druids on the shores of the Menai Straits, as Tacitus describes. Moreover copying from one text to another brought the Druids by report into the writings of those who had not travelled in Celtic lands. Provided it is remembered that Posidonius was looking at the Druids hopefully for confirmation of his ideas of a golden age of innocence, and that Caesar was thinking primarily about his political prestige in Rome, the writings of the Posidonian group give us a remarkably objective picture of the Druids, and of the Celtic culture of which they were an expression.

This culture was multiple and diverse, rural and uncentralized. There were no formal buildings for religious purposes. The teaching of novices for the priesthood took place in lonely forest clearings which were the usual Celtic sanctuaries. Oral teaching and learning by heart of sacred verses was given by Druids to the sons of the warrior nobility entering for instruction into the priesthood, whose status must always have been high. Strabo and Posidonius distinguish between three classes: the bards, the seers, and the Druids proper; Caesar merely between two: the knights and the Druids. The diviners or seers seem to have drawn auguries from the sacrifices performed by the Druids, while the bards were poets or composers of eulogy or satire, as well as the singers of these poems for ceremonial or entertainment purposes. Druids may in some circumstances have acted as diviners, but their function was distinct from that of the bards. All matters of knowledge, sacred and profane, were the province of the Druids, who also wielded considerable juridicial power as "the most just of men." Settlement of property disputes, of boundaries and the judging of all crimes and controversies was carried out by them. They could bar from attendance at sacrifices any individual or tribe who did not accept their rulings, thus making them outcasts without religious or legal status.

It is hardly realistic to exculpate the Druides from participation, probably active, in both the beliefs and practices involved in human sacrifice (which after all had only been brought to an end in the civilized Roman world in the early first century B.C.). Caesar writes of the use of "huge figures woven out of twigs whose limbs they fill with living men and set on fire"; Strabo confirms this strange rite, which remains unexplained and unparalleled and has caught the imaginations of all who have subsequently written on Druids. Other forms of human sacrifice included impaling or shooting to death by arrows, and Diodorus and Strabo describe how victims were stabbed in the back and omens deduced from their death throes.

Our information on Druid ceremonies mainly centres on sacrifice. Pliny gives us the only detailed account of a Druid ceremony, which was concerned with the growth of mistletoe on an oak tree, a circumstance of rare occurrence. The time chosen for the rite was the sixth day of the moon and preparations were made for a feast and a sacrifice of two white bulls. A Druid in a white robe climbed the tree and cut the branch of mistletoe with a golden sickle. The branch was caught on a white cloak as it fell. The bulls were sacrificed. The golden sickle is inexplicable: if it really existed it would have been unable to cut the tough stem of mistletoe: gilded bronze is more likely. Pliny's account of the ritual necessity of gathering the plant *samolus* left-handed and fasting, and of plucking *selago* without using an iron knife, barefoot, and with the right hand through the left sleeve of a white tunic, are performances of private magic rather than public ceremonies.

Druidic philosophy or doctrine is harder to reconstruct than their ritual observances; they are unlikely to have held the coherent body of dogma attributed to them by Posidonius, to whom the Druids are leaders of humanity particularly endowed with the *Logos* principle, and holding as chief tenets the immortality of the soul and the indestructibility of the universe—although from time to time it is temporarily consumed by fire or water. Yet Posidonius was one of the most acute observers of antiquity, and Strabo and Mela confirm that the Druids had knowledge "of the magnitude and form of the earth and the world;" also their belief in successive transformations of an eternal matter and in the alternate triumph of the two elements, fire and water. Caesar and Mela state that, "They profess to know the motions of the heavens and the stars and their movement, the size of the universe and of the earth." The Druids in Diodorus are "skilled in the divine nature," and are able to communicate with the gods.

The item of Druidic belief that struck the classical writers most forcibly was that of literal, personal immortality. In Posidonius, as quoted by Diodorus, the Celts held that "the souls of men are immortal and that after a definite number of years they live a second life when the soul passes to another body." From this, Diodorus continues, followed the idea of the redemption of one life by another, while Caesar makes the chief point of doctrine that "men's souls do not suffer death, but after death pass from the one to the other." Ammianus, Valerius Maximus and Diodorus associate the belief in immortality with the Pythagorean theory of metempsychosis— equating the Celtic doctrine with the beliefs of Pythagoras—or making the Druids "members of the intimate fellowship of the Pythagorean faith." This is hardly conceivable, although it is reasonably likely that similar beliefs were held by the Pythagoreans and the Druids.

The references in the classical authors on which our knowledge of the very existence of the Druids is based range in date from around the end of the third century B.C. to the fourth century A.D., and relate to Western Europe and to Britain. The earliest vernacular texts in Old Irish represent written recensions of an oral tradition dating from somewhere shortly before the fifth century A.D., and relate only to Ireland. There is therefore a virtual continuity over five hundred years, so far as actual chronology is concerned, but an abrupt shift of scene between the comments of the Greek and Roman writers and the indigenous Celtic record. But all the literary sources are set within a consistent framework which can be historically, linguistically and ethnographically defined as that of the ancient Celts.

To place the Druids in their proper setting therefore we must form a picture of the Celtic world to which they belonged—a self-sufficient and remarkably homogeneous, iron-using, barbarian economy, based on its flocks and herds and its ploughlands, with a warrior-aristocracy supporting skilled artists and craftsmen, the whole economic and social structure dependent for its strength and inspiration on the ritual, magic and religious beliefs controlled and directed by the Druids.

SOURCES
OF THE ILLUSTRATIONS

Frontispiece : Boadicea contemplating suicide. Mary Evans Picture Library, London.

1. Boadicea the formidable matron, from Sammes *Britannia Antiqua*, 1676. British Museum, London.
2. Statue of Boadicea and her daughters, sculpted by Thornycroft, nineteenth century. Mansell Collection, London.
3. Title page of *Boadicia a Tragedy*, by Mr. Glover, published in 1753. British Museum, London.
4. Caractacus before Claudius, early nineteenth century engraving. Mansell Collection, London.
5. Boadicea haranguing the Iceni, nineteenth century painting by H.C. Selous. Mansell Collection, London.
6. A print of Mrs. Hunter as Boadicea, 1778. Mary Evans Picture Library, London.
7. Boadicea, aquatint of the nineteenth century. Mansell Collection, London.
8. The Desborough mirror. British Museum, London.
9. A funerary head from a grave at Towchester, Northants. British Museum, London.
10. Bronze head of the Emperor Claudius, found in the river Alde at Saxmundham, Suffolk. British Museum, London.
11. Limestone head of mid first century A.D. The City Museum, Gloucester.
12. Reconstruction of a British chariot based on material from Llyn Cerrig Bach in Anglesey. National Museum of Wales, Cardiff.
13. Bridle bits from British horse chariots. British Museum, London.
14. Coins used by the Iceni. British Museum, London.
15. Romano-British bronze figure of a ploughman with oxen, found at Piercebridge, Durham. British Museum, London.
16. British bronze shield boss, found in the Thames at Battersea. British Museum, London.
17. The Snettisham gold torque. British Museum, London.
18. Bronze statue of Nero, found at Barking Hall, Suffolk. British Museum, London.
19. Roman coins bearing the heads of Nero and Julius Caesar. British Museum, London.
20. Toys from the grave of a Roman child, first century A.D. Colchester and Essex Museum.
21. Map showing the limits of Roman advance in Britain in 60 A.D. Anne Cope.
22. The tombstone of Longinus, Colchester Museum, Colchester.

23. Roman soldiers in combat, detail from Trajan's column. Mansell Collection, London.
24. British iron dagger and bronze sheath, found in the Thames at Cookham, Berkshire. British Museum, London.
25. Tombstone of Roman centurion, Facilis. Colchester Museum, Colchester.
26. Pottery antefix of the XX Legion. British Museum, London.
27. Reconstruction of Roman Colchester. *Illustrated London News*, July 15th, 1950.
28. Reconstruction of the Temple of Claudius at Colchester. Colchester Museum, Colchester.
29. Painting of London as it may have looked in the time of Boadicea. The London Museum, London.
30. A contemporary view of Watling Street. Aerofilms Limited, London.
31. Bronze equestrian statue of Nero. Mansell Collection, London.
32. The Praetorian Guard. The Louvre, Paris.
33. A Gallic forest god. Musée des Antiquités Nationales, St.-Germain-en-Laye.